Oracle8*i* Internal Services
for Waits, Latches, Locks, and Memory

Oracle8*i* Internal Services
for Waits, Latches, Locks, and Memory

Steve Adams

O'REILLY®

Beijing · Cambridge · Farnham · Köln · Paris · Sebastopol · Taipei · Tokyo

Oracle8i Internal Services for Waits, Latches, Locks, and Memory
by Steve Adams

Published by O'Reilly & Associates, Inc., 101 Morris Street, Sebastopol, CA 95472.

Editor: Deborah Russell

Production Editor: Colleen Gorman

Printing History:

>   October 1999:   First Edition.

ISBN: 1-56592-598-X   [1/01]
[M]

Table of Contents

Preface

A few years ago, I set my heart on researching and writing a truly advanced Oracle performance-tuning book. Soon, I had a detailed outline running to more than thirty pages. But when I started to write, I began to realize how much I had yet to learn about Oracle. Each chapter was going to require considerably more research than I had at first imagined. In particular, I began to realize that an understanding of some aspects of Oracle internals would be vital to my quest. So I began to learn what I could of Oracle internals, starting with the X$ tables.

If I had known then what I know now, about how vast an undertaking I was commencing, I would probably never have attempted it. And many times I would have given up in despair, except for the encouragement of my friends. They always believed that I could comprehend the incomprehensible and construct a coherent understanding of how Oracle works and should be tuned. It has been somewhat like trying to determine the exact shape of an iceberg by walking all over it and taking careful measurements of subsurface vibrations.

Why This Book?

My advanced Oracle performance-tuning book is still a dream. This little book is something else: an introduction to Oracle internals. It builds the foundation necessary for advanced performance tuning by explaining some of the basic aspects of Oracle internals in detail.

Here you will find many of the undocumented system statistics explained. You will learn how to gather additional statistics from the X$ tables. Your understanding of how Oracle works will be deepened with clear explanations of many of Oracle's internal data structures and algorithms. You will be alerted to potential performance problems that are not mentioned in the documentation. And you will expand your repertoire of tuning solutions and troubleshooting techniques by learning how to use numerous hidden parameters and other undocumented features.

Warnings

The kind of Oracle internals information I've included in this book is not readily available to customers. Because I have never been an Oracle insider, the material in this book has had to be compiled the hard way. I began by studying the structure and contents of the X$ tables, and poring over trace files. I then formulated hypotheses and tested them. Because of this approach, it is likely that some of my conclusions about how things work are wrong, and that some of my suggestions are misguided, or applicable only under limited conditions. So, the onus is on you to test everything for yourself. If you find any errors, please email me so that they can be corrected (see "Comments and Questions").

You should also note that this book goes boldly where Oracle Support fears to tread. I explain and at times recommend the use of various undocumented features that I find essential to advanced performance tuning. However, Oracle has chosen to leave those same features undocumented—presumably with valid reasons. So please don't expect Oracle to assist you in their use. Try them by all means, but if you have a problem, quit. Don't bother Oracle Support about it.

Finally, please note that this book is oriented towards Oracle*8i*, release 8.1. Although most of the material is applicable to earlier releases as well, some of it is not. In particular, there have been major changes in Oracle Parallel Server in both the 8.0 and 8.1 releases, and a number of the parameters have been hidden in release 8.1.

Audience for This Book

This book is intended for Oracle database administrators (DBAs) and developers who need to understand Oracle performance in detail. Although the information is advanced, the presentation is easy to follow. Anyone who is familiar with the basics of the Oracle architecture and has an aptitude for performance tuning will be able to appreciate everything in this book. However, seasoned veterans will no doubt appreciate it the most.

About the APT Scripts

This book makes a number of references to APT scripts. APT stands for *Advanced Performance Tuning*. It is merely my personal toolkit of Oracle performance tuning scripts. The scripts referred to in this book can be obtained from O'Reilly's web site or from my own (see "Comments and Questions"). APT is not a commercial product, and I do not warrant that the scripts are error-free. But you are free to use them, or glean from them what you may.

Conventions Used in This Book

The following conventions are used in this book:

Italic
> Used for the names of files, scripts, latches, statistics, and wait events; also used for emphasis and for new terms

`Constant width`
> Used for examples and literals

UPPERCASE
> Used for Oracle SQL keywords, initialization parameters, and the names of tables, views, columns, packages, and procedures

Comments and Questions

Please address comments and questions concerning this book to the publisher:

> O'Reilly & Associates, Inc.
> 101 Morris Street
> Sebastopol, CA 95472
> 800-998-9938 (in the U.S. or Canada)
> 707-829-0515 (international or local)
> 707-829-0104 (fax)

You can also send us messages electronically (*booktech@oreilly.com*). For corrections and amplifications to this book, as well as for copies of the APT scripts referred to in the book, check out O'Reilly & Associates' online catalog at:

> *http://www.oreilly.com/catalog/orinternals/*

The APT scripts can also be obtained from my web site at:

> *http://www.ixora.com.au/*

You can also contact me directly at:

steve.adams@ixora.com.au

See the advertisements at the end of the book for information about all of O'Reilly & Associates' online services.

Acknowledgments

My partner in this project, as in all things, is my wife, Alison Adams. If you appreciate this book, then it is to Alison that your thanks are due. Much as I have tried to limit the impact of researching and writing this book on my family, this project has deprived Alison and our young children, Jennifer, Stephanie, and David of much time that would otherwise have been spent with them.

I would also like to thank Guy Harrison, who first got me interested in Oracle performance, Jonathan Lewis, from whom I have learned the most, Dave Ensor, who corrected my understanding of immediate gets, and Jared Still, who has always been willing to run tests to check my ideas. Thank you, friends, for your help with reviewing the first draft of each chapter, and for your constant encouragement. Thanks also to the many people with whom I have interacted on the Internet mailing lists and discussion forums over the years. You have provided a wealth of vicarious experience and sustained encouragement in my quest to understand Oracle.

Thanks to the team at O'Reilly & Associates for agreeing to publish this book, and for their work in preparing it, and thanks to the team of final reviewers: Jonathan Gennick, Amjad Daoud, and Anjo Kolk.

1

Introduction

Why are people so intensely interested in Oracle internals? Partly because internals information can be useful for tuning and troubleshooting. But also because Oracle Corporation has kept most of the internals secret, while revealing just enough to tantalize.

In fact, Oracle internals information is needed only for advanced performance tuning. It's true that basic application tuning is the kind of tuning that's most often needed, and the kind that has the biggest impact. Nevertheless, there are times when advanced performance tuning is necessary, and that is when you need a deep understanding of how Oracle works. This book provides some of the foundations for that understanding.

To appreciate the contribution that this book makes, and to put it in context, you need to have a basic understanding of the layers of the Oracle kernel.

The Oracle Kernel Layers

The Oracle kernel is comprised of layers; the main layers are shown in Figure 1-1. Each layer depends upon the services of the layers below it, and may call any of them directly, in any order. However, control is never passed up the stack, except when returning from a call.

The one apparent exception to this rule is that the data layer and the transaction layer sometimes need to perform recursive transactions for tasks such as index block splits or extent space management, and recursive calls are needed for tasks such as trigger execution or SQL statement execution from within stored program units. However, instead of calling back to the kernel execution or compilation layer from within the same session or call context, a separate context is established and the stack is reentered from the top layer.

Oracle Call Interface	OCI
User Program Interface	UPI

◀─────────────────────────────────────▶ *Net8*

Oracle Program Interface	OPI
Compilation Layer	KK
Execution Layer	KX
Distributed Execution Layer	K2
Network Program Interface	NPI
Security Layer	KZ
Query Layer	KQ
Recursive Program Interface	RPI
Access Layer	KA
Data Layer	KD
Transaction Layer	KT
Cache Layer	KC
Services Layer	KS
Lock Management Layer	KJ
Generic Layer	KG
Operating System Dependencies	S

Figure 1-1. The Oracle kernel layers

Each layer has a short name, or abbreviation, that is used as a prefix to the names of its modules. For example, KC is the short name for the kernel cache layer. These short names are shown in Figure 1-1 and in the following list. Similarly, each of the modules that comprise the layers has a short name too. For example, KCR is the redo management module within the cache layer. These module names are prefixed to the names of their data structures and function calls. For example, KCRFAL is the redo allocation latch. This naming convention makes Oracle's names seem rather cryptic and formidable at first, but they soon become surprisingly easy to recognize and a great aid to understanding. Nevertheless, you will be pleased to know that this book uses the verbose names in preference to their somewhat cryptic alternatives.

The Oracle call interface (OCI)

The Oracle call interface is the lowest level at which client programs are intended to interact with Oracle. This interface is well documented and provides access to most of the functionality of Oracle, including advanced features such as object navigation, and sophisticated transaction and session control. Applications with advanced requirements have to use OCI directly, in order to access the features that are not available in Oracle's other development tools.

The user program interface (UPI)
OCI is based on the user program interface. There are some UPI facilities that are not yet available via OCI, and so some of the Oracle tools actually call this interface directly. Precompiler programs also call the user program interface, but indirectly via the SQLLIB library, which is an undocumented alternative to OCI.

The Oracle program interface (OPI)
The user program interface is the lowest layer of the client-side call stack, and the Oracle program interface is the highest layer of the server-side call stack. In most configurations, Net8 bridges the gap between UPI and OPI. However, in single-task executables there is no gap, and the UPI calls correspond directly to OPI calls.

The compilation layer (KK)
This is the top layer of the Oracle kernel proper. This layer is responsible for the parsing and optimization of SQL statements and for the compilation of PL/SQL program units.

The execution layer (KX)
This layer handles the binding and execution of SQL statements and PL/SQL program units. It is also responsible for the execution of recursive calls for trigger execution, and for the execution of SQL statements within PL/SQL program units.

The distributed execution layer (K2)
The distributed execution layer establishes the transaction branches for distributed transactions, and handles the management of the two-phase commit protocol.

The network program interface (NPI)
When remote objects are referenced in a SQL statement, the network program interface sends the decomposed statement components to the remote database instances and receives the data in return.

The security layer (KZ)
This layer is called by the compilation and execution layers to validate the required object and system privileges.

The query layer (KQ)
This layer provides rows to the higher layers. In particular, the query layer is responsible for caching rows from the data dictionary, for use by the security and compilation layers.

The recursive program interface (RPI)

The recursive program interface is used to populate the dictionary cache from the data dictionary. Row cache recursive SQL statements are executed in a separate call context, but are not parsed and optimized in the compilation layer.

The access layer (KA)

The access layer is responsible for access to database segments. This is the first layer of the lower half of the kernel.

The data layer (KD)

This layer is responsible for the management and interpretation of data within the blocks of database segments such as tables, clusters, and indexes.

The transaction layer (KT)

This layer is responsible for the allocation of transactions to rollback segments, interested transaction list changes within data blocks, changes to rollback segment blocks for undo generation, transaction control facilities such as savepoints, and read consistency. The transaction layer is also responsible for space management, both at the level of segment free lists and at the level of tablespace extent allocation.

The cache layer (KC)

The cache layer manages the database buffer cache. It uses operating system dependent facilities for data file I/O, provides concurrency control facilities for local access to the cache buffers, and provides parallel cache management (PCM) instance locking facilities for Oracle parallel server. The other main responsibility of the cache layer is the control of redo generation into the log buffer, and the writing of redo to the log files. The cache layer also caches control file information.

The services layer (KS)

The services layer provides low-level services that are used by all the higher layers, such as error handling, debugging, and tracing facilities, as well as parameter control and memory services. In particular, the service layer is responsible for generic concurrency control facilities such as latches, event waits, enqueue locks, and instance locks. This layer is also responsible for the management of the data structures for background and user processes and sessions, as well as state objects, inter-process messages, and system statistics.

The lock management layer (KJ)

This layer is responsible for the locking used for synchronization and communication between the instances of a parallel server database.

The generic layer (KG)

> The generic layer provides management for the generic data structures that are used by the higher layers, such as linked lists. Of particular interest are the library cache and the memory allocation heaps used for the shared pool and session memory.

The operating system dependencies (S)

> Oracle uses operating system facilities for I/O, process scheduling, memory management, and other operations. The implementation details are operating system dependent, and so these details are isolated into a separate layer.

The Kernel Services

This book covers the kernel services for waits, latches, locks, and memory. Although there is relatively little you can do to tune these services themselves, you will need to understand them when you tune any other part of Oracle.

Chapter 2, Waits

> The wait statistics are the most important Oracle statistics for advanced performance tuning. This chapter explains how to gather and use these statistics.

Chapter 3, Latches

> Oracle makes extensive use of latches, and advanced performance tuning often involves the prevention of latch contention. This chapter provides a foundation for such tuning by explaining how latches are used.

Chapter 4, Locks

> Oracle uses many types of locks. This chapter explains how locks are used, and how to diagnose locking problems.

Chapter 5, Instance Locks

> Oracle parallel server technology adds an extra dimension to Oracle tuning. This chapter explains how parallel server locking is implemented, and what the statistics mean.

Chapter 6, Memory

> This chapter explains how Oracle's internal memory management works. I pay particular attention to the inner workings of the shared pool, and to assessing whether it is sized correctly.

Although there is much more to Oracle internals than this small book covers, these chapters provide the foundation that you need for advanced performance tuning.

2

Waits

In an Oracle instance many processes (or threads of a single process) work together. To work together, they must communicate, and one of main ways that they communicate is via semaphores. A *semaphore* is a signal. It is somewhat like a railway signal that tells trains whether to stop and wait, and when to go. Oracle server processes often need to stop and wait:

* Sometimes because a resource is not available

* Sometimes because they have no work to do

* Sometimes because they need to wait for another server process to perform a prerequisite task

Semaphores allow Oracle server processes to stop and wait, and then to be notified when they should resume processing.

Semaphores

There is a semaphore for every Oracle server process. Processes wait on their semaphore when they need to wait for a resource, or need work to do, or need work to be done. When the resource has been freed, or when there is work to do, or when the prerequisite work has been done, then their semaphore is posted as a signal to stop waiting.

For example, LGWR (the Log Writer process) may be waiting on its semaphore for work to do, while a user process may be copying redo information into the redo log buffer. When the user commits, LGWR must write the redo and commit marker to the log file while the user waits. To achieve this, the user process posts LGWR's semaphore to signal that it can stop waiting for work to do, as some work is now available. The user process then waits on its own semaphore. When the log file I/O has completed, LGWR posts the semaphore of the user process to signal that it can now begin its next transaction, because the commit operation has completed. LGWR then waits on its own semaphore again, because it has no more work to do.

For another example, process A may need to update a row, but find that process B has not yet committed an earlier update to the same row. Process A must wait for process B to commit. To achieve this, process A will wait on its semaphore. When process B commits, it will post process A's semaphore to signal that it can now proceed with its update.

Semaphore Facilities

Semaphores are an operating system facility. When an Oracle process is waiting on its semaphore, the operating system will not schedule it to run on a CPU. In operating system terms, it is blocked, not runnable. When the semaphore is posted, the operating system status of the process is changed from blocked to runnable, and the process will be scheduled to run as soon as possible.

Some operating systems support more than one type of semaphore. System V semaphores are the most common. The semaphore data structures for System V semaphores form a fixed array in kernel memory sized by the SEMMNS kernel parameter. To post a semaphore or wait on a semaphore, processes must use the *semop()* system call. Because they are implemented in the operating system kernel, System V semaphores suffer from unnecessarily high system call context switch overheads and poor scalability due to serialization requirements for access to the kernel data structures.

For better performance and scalability, an alternative set of semaphore operations is supported on several operating systems. These are implemented in a pseudo device driver, called a post-wait driver. The data structures for these semaphores reside in user memory, rather than kernel memory, and can therefore be manipulated by the pseudo device driver running in user context. This reduces the number of system call context switches, and improves scalability, but it is operating system specific.

The POSIX real-time extensions subcommittee has identified the need for a standards-compliant user memory semaphore facility. The POSIX.1b standard (formerly POSIX.4) defines both the interface and implementation requirements for such a semaphore facility that is elegant and efficient, not to mention portable. POSIX.1b semaphores are now available on many operating systems.

Which semaphore facility Oracle uses is operating system and release specific. If your Oracle installation guide has instructions about setting the SEMMNS kernel parameter, that means System V semaphores will be used by default. Unfortunately, this is still the case on a large number of operating systems. Incidentally, the prevalent recommendation to set SEMMNS to 200, without regard for the projected number of Oracle processes, or the requirements of other system and application software, is ill-conceived. You must allow one semaphore for each Oracle server process, in addition to other requirements, as explained more fully in Table 2-1.

You should also be aware that on some platforms each Oracle instance requires its semaphores to be allocated in a single semaphore set. So the SEMMNI parameter need only allow one semaphore identifier per instance, and SEMMSL (if defined) must be no less than the largest PROCESSES parameter that might be required for any instance. This is necessary to enable vector posts. Vector posts may be used, mainly by the key background processes, LGWR and DBWn, to post multiple waiting processes in a single semaphore operation. The use of vector posts is dependent on the setting of the _USE_VECTOR_POSTS parameter.

Hidden Parameters

Parameters that begin with an underscore, such as _USE_VECTOR_ POSTS, are hidden parameters. You will not find them in V$PARAMETER, or see them with the SHOW PARAMETERS command, because they are hidden. You certainly will not find them explained in the Oracle documentation, because they are undocumented. You can, however, get their descriptions with the APT script *hidden_parameters.sql* and check their values with the script *all_parameters.sql.*

Some hidden parameters are operating system specific. Some are needed only in unusual recovery situations. Some are used to disable or enable new features. And many are related to obscure performance issues. As with all undocumented features, hidden parameters may disappear or change in a future release. You should therefore use them as a last resort, and only after checking with Oracle Support, and documenting the issues fully for your successor.

Further, if the SEMMNU kernel parameter is defined for your operating system, it should be greater than the projected number of concurrent semaphore operations system-wide. For systems with many semaphore client processes, the default may be inadequate. If so, semaphore operations will fail intermittently at periods of peak activity and return the ORA-7264 or ORA-7265 errors. To avoid this, the SEMMNU parameter must be at least equal to the number of CPUs plus the peak length of the CPU run queues.

Table 2-1. System V Semaphore Parameters

Parameter	Description
SEMMNS	The number of semaphores in the system. In addition to the requirements of the operating system and other software, you should allow at least one semaphore for each Oracle server process—that is, the sum of the setting of the PROCESSES parameter for all instances on the system. If the semaphore clients are not always shut down and started up in strict sequence, then an extra allowance at least equal to the largest single requirement is recommended. Further, the kernel parameter controlling the maximum number of simultaneous processes owned by a single named user (often MAXUP) should be at least equal to the SEMMNS setting, with an allowance for other administrative processes owned by the "oracle" user that do not require semaphores. However, this parameter should not be so large as to allow the risk of another user creating so many processes that the kernel process table would be completely filled. Therefore, the kernel parameter controlling the maximum number of simultaneous processes for all users (often NPROC) should be at least three times the value of SEMMNS.
SEMMSL	The size limit for a single semaphore set. This parameter is not defined on some operating systems. Where it is defined, and where Oracle requires all the semaphores for an instance to be allocated in a single semaphore set, this parameter must be at least equal to the largest PROCESSES parameter required for any instance.
SEMMNI	The number of semaphore set identifiers in the system. In addition to the requirements of the operating system and other software, you should allow one identifier per instance, or more if the SEMMSL parameter is set such that multiple semaphore sets will be required for any instance.
SEMMNU	The number of semaphore undo structures in the system. Undo structures are used to recover the kernel semaphore data structures in the event of the unexpected death of a process during a semaphore operation. SEMMNU should be greater than the peak number of running and runnable processes.

If Oracle uses System V semaphores on your operating system by default, but also supports the use of a post-wait driver, then you should use the post-wait driver instead. This normally involves setting the USE_POST_WAIT_DRIVER parameter to TRUE, and it is sometimes necessary to set the POST_WAIT_DEVICE parameter as well. Please consult your Oracle installation guide, because the instructions are operating system and release dependent.

If your installation guide makes no mention of setting kernel semaphore parameters or of a post-wait driver, the selection and configuration of the semaphore facility for your operating system is automatic.

Note that the semaphore parameters are operating system kernel parameters and cannot be set in the Oracle initialization parameter file (*INIT.ORA*).

Scheduling Latencies

When a process is posted, its operating system status is changed from blocked to runnable. However, that does not mean it will be scheduled to run on a CPU immediately. It must wait at least until the operating system's process scheduler is next run, and possibly longer if there are higher priority processes waiting to run. The delay from when a process is posted until it begins running is called the *scheduling latency*. Scheduling latencies contribute to Oracle response times, as illustrated in Figure 2-1, and so minimizing scheduling latencies is an important part of performance tuning.

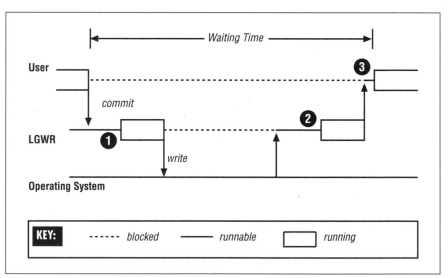

Figure 2-1. The three scheduling latencies for a commit

Many operating system scheduling algorithms adjust the execution priority of processes in proportion to the amount of CPU time that they have consumed recently. In very busy Oracle environments, this has the unfortunate effect of degrading the execution priority of key background processes, such as LGWR, DBWn, LCKn, and LMDn. This causes an increase in scheduling latencies for those processes, and can in the extreme make the entire instance bottleneck on the services of the affected background processes.

Some operating systems support multiple scheduling algorithms. Where possible, you should choose a scheduling algorithm that does not degrade the execution priority of processes in this way. Failing that, your operating system may provide a priority fixing facility. If the execution priority of a process is fixed, it will not degrade. In some cases, priority fixing is available to all users, and Oracle uses it automatically. In other cases, it is only available to the system administrator, and specially privileged users. If so, the "oracle" user must be granted this privilege, or the system administrator must start the Oracle instance from a fixed priority command shell, so that all Oracle processes will run with fixed priority.

Where priority fixing is not available, you may be able to obtain equivalent relief from the priority degradation mechanism by artificially raising the execution priority of the key background processes, or even running them in the real-time priority class. You may feel reluctant to do this, on the basis that Oracle has often recommended that all Oracle processes should run at the same priority. The rationale for this recommendation is to prevent the possibility of a low-priority process holding a critical resource but being unable to free it because of CPU starvation, while other high-priority processes try repeatedly to obtain that resource. However, this rationale scarcely applies to raising the priority of the background processes. These processes will soon sleep if the resources they require are not available, and beyond that will only consume CPU time in proportion to the amount of work being done by the rest of the instance. So, there is no risk of CPU starvation for other Oracle processes.

Timeouts

Oracle server processes are never willing to wait indefinitely, lest they never be posted and wait forever. Fortunately, semaphore waits can be interrupted. So before an Oracle process begins to wait on its semaphore, it arranges for its sleep to be interrupted by setting an alarm clock, or *timeout*. If the process is posted, it switches the alarm clock off and then continues processing. However, if the timeout expires, the wait is interrupted by a SIGALRM signal. The process then has the opportunity to reassess the situation and decide whether it wants to continue to wait.

For example, a process waiting for an enqueue lock may perform dead-lock detection when its wait times out. If a deadlock is discovered, the statement will be rolled back and an exception will be raised, but if not, the process will set a new timeout and will begin to wait on its sema-phore again.

It sometimes happens that a process is posted very shortly before its timeout is due to expire, and the alarm goes off just as the process is trying to switch it off. In this case, the Oracle process concerned will write a message to its trace file:

```
Ignoring SIGALRM
```

If you find some trace files with this message, it is nothing to be alarmed about. It merely tells you that waiting processes are sometimes not being posted as quickly as you might wish, and that is something you ought to be aware of anyway from the wait statistics.

Wait Statistics

The Oracle wait statistics are pure gold—but not to be overvalued. Many types of performance problems are easy to identify from the wait statis-tics. If Oracle is waiting extensively for resources such as latches, free cache buffers, enqueue locks, and so on, then the wait statistics can both identify and quantify the problem. With experience, you may also be able to use the wait statistics to identify network and disk performance prob-lems. The wait statistics also provide valuable feedback on attempts to resolve such problems.

But if your application is doing more parsing, or more disk I/O than necessary for its workload, then the wait statistics cannot help you. They will appear to give your instance a clean bill of health, and rightly so. The wait statistics are only able to reveal inefficiencies at the database server level and below. So they are silent about application-level performance problems that increase the load on the database server but do not cause it to work inefficiently.

However, you should already have addressed all the application perfor-mance issues before considering database server tuning in detail. If so, the wait statistics can have full value for database server tuning. But they can only have full value if the waits are timed.

Timed Statistics

Waits are timed if and only if the TIMED_STATISTICS parameter is set to TRUE. Let me endorse what others have said before, that the overhead of timed statistics is negligible. If you need to convince yourself, use the SET TIMING ON command in SQL*Plus to measure the elapsed time of a benchmark query. Use an otherwise idle system and take ten or more measurements with and without timed statistics. You will be hard pressed to discern any significant difference.

Without timed statistics, Oracle records the reason for each wait before it begins to wait, and when the wait is over, it records whether it timed out. But with timed statistics enabled, Oracle checks the time just before and after each wait, and also records the time waited. The time waited is recorded in hundredths of a second—that is, centiseconds.

 Bug 918002 can inhibit SQL statement sharing and cause latch contention in release 8.1.5 if TIMED_STATISTICS or SQL_TRACE are used. Bug 1210242 can cause the same performance problem under release 8.1.6 if both facilities are used concurrently.

Wait Types

V$SYSTEM_EVENT shows the total number of waits and timeouts, and the total waiting time recorded for each type of event, accumulated for all processes over the life of the instance. It is normal to order the events waited for in descending order of the total time waited, as an indicator of the potential severity of each type of wait.

However, the total time waited is really only meaningful for those that indicate waiting for resources. If processes have been waiting because they have no work to do, then the time waited is immaterial. If they have been waiting for routine operations, such as disk I/O, then the total time waited will depend on the workload. In such cases, the average time waited is much more interesting than the total time waited.

This classification of wait types into idle waits, routine waits, and resource waits is vital to a correct understanding of the wait statistics. Accordingly, APT has separate scripts for resource waits and routine waits, and ignores idle waits altogether. The *routine_waits.sql* script shows only the average time waited for each type of routine wait. The *resource_waits.sql* script (see Example 2-1) shows the types of resources waited for in descending order of the total time waited, but also shows the average time waited.

Example 2-1. Sample Output from resource_waits.sql

```
SQL> @resource_waits

EVENT                                      TIME_WAITED AVERAGE_WAIT
------------------------------------------ ----------- ------------
write complete waits                           3816218       212.02
buffer busy waits                              1395921        21.79
enqueue                                         503217       529.15
log file switch completion                      144263        90.11
latch free                                       31173         0.61
free buffer waits                                19352       302.38
row cache lock                                     876        73.00
library cache pin                                  131        18.71
library cache load lock                             29         2.64
non-routine log file syncs                           0         2.32
```

The average time waited reported by *resource_waits.sql* is not what you
might expect. Because of timeouts, a single logical wait for a resource
may be reported as a series of distinct waits, each of which would have
timed out, except the last. The number of logical waits is approximately
the number of times the waiting process was posted to end its wait—that
is, the number of distinct waits, minus the number of waits that timed out.
The average time waited for each logical wait is a better indication of the
time taken to resolve resource waits, than the average time for each
component wait. Therefore, that is what this script reports for all resource
waits except *latch free* waits. It is normal for *latch free* waits to time out,
because latch wait posting is the exception, not the rule. Also, apart from
latch contention, it is normal for the latch to be obtained after a timeout.
So the average time waited for each distinct wait is a better indication of
the duration of *latch free* waits.

Session Waits

V$SESSION_EVENT shows the wait statistics for each live session.
Although waits affect processes rather than sessions, they are recorded
against sessions because sessions can migrate between processes (as in
Multi-Threaded Server configurations). The cumulative session wait statistics have two main uses.

First, if a particular user reports an episode of poor performance, then the
wait statistics for that session can be examined to diagnose that user's
problem. The APT script called *session_times.sql* (see Example 2-2) shows
the waiting time accumulated by the session for each type of event waited
for, together with the amount of CPU time consumed by that session. This
makes it easy to see whether the session has been working or waiting,
and if it has been waiting, what it has been waiting for.

Example 2-2. Sample Output from session_times.sql

```
SQL> @session_times

Enter SID: 29


EVENT                                                       TIME_WAITED
--------------------------------------------------------   -----------
SQL*Net message from client                                    2954196
CPU used by this session                                       1657275
db file sequential read                                         246759
write complete waits                                            139698
buffer busy waits                                                61832
log file sync                                                    32601
enqueue                                                           9576
log file switch completion                                        3530
SQL*Net message to client                                         2214
db file scattered read                                            1879
SQL*Net more data to client                                        952
SQL*Net more data from client                                      908
latch free                                                         840
free buffer waits                                                  100
buffer deadlock                                                     57
row cache lock                                                       1
SQL*Net break/reset to client                                        0
```

Second, if there has been extensive waiting for a particular type of resource, then the session wait statistics can be used to determine which of the sessions that are still connected have contributed to or been affected by the problem. The APT script for this job is called *resource_ waiters.sql*. It shows the breakdown by session of the waiting time for the resource type in question. The total waiting time for sessions that are no longer active is also shown. For example, if there have been a large number of *buffer busy waits*, then looking at the session wait statistics may reveal whether the problem has been widespread, or confined to just a few sessions.

Wait Parameters

The wait statistics are very useful because they tell you which sessions have been waiting, and which types of resources they have been waiting for. They may have been waiting for latches, database blocks, enqueue locks, or other resource types. Knowing which type can direct your tuning efforts. But the wait parameters are even more valuable than the wait statistics. They can tell you exactly which resource—which latch, which database block, or which enqueue lock—is being waited for. The wait statistics merely put you in the right neighborhood, but the wait parameters can focus your attention on the right spot.

Unfortunately, the wait parameters are hard to catch. They can be seen fleetingly in V$SESSION_WAIT. This view shows the wait parameters for the current or most recent wait for each session, as well as the duration of the wait, if known. However, querying V$SESSION_WAIT takes a long time relative to the length of most waits. If you query this view twice in quick succession and look at the SEQ# column, which is incremented for each distinct wait, it is not uncommon to notice that many event waits have been missed in each active session between the two queries. It is also rather expensive to query V$SESSION_WAIT repeatedly in quick succession, and so it is of limited usefulness for watching wait parameters.

Fortunately, the wait parameters can also be seen in trace files produced by the new DBMS_SUPPORT package, or by the underlying event 10046. This trace is the same as that produced by the SQL_TRACE facility but also includes a line for each wait, including the wait parameters.

For example, if there appears to be a problem with *buffer busy waits*, then you can enable this trace for a while in the most heavily affected sessions with the APT script *trace_waits.sql*. It is then just a matter of extracting the buffer busy wait lines from the trace files, and examining the wait parameters to find the file and block numbers of the blocks being waited for. In the case of *buffer busy waits,* the file and block numbers are parameters p1 and p2. This is illustrated in Example 2-3.

Example 2-3. Sample Dialog from trace_waits.sql

```
SQL> @trace_waits

This script uses event 10046, level 8 to trace the event waits in
the top N sessions affected by waits for a particular resource.

Select sessions waiting for: buffer busy waits
Number of sessions to trace: 5
Seconds to leave tracing on: 900

Tracing ... Please wait ...

PL/SQL procedure successfully completed.

SQL> exit
$ cd udump
$ grep 'buffer busy waits' ora_*.trc |
> sed -e 's/.*p1=/  file /' -e 's/ p2=/  block /' -e 's/ p3.*//' |
> sort |
> uniq -c |
> sort -nr |
> head -5
   42    file 2     block 1036
   12    file 24    block 3
   10    file 2     block 1252
```

Example 2-3. Sample Dialog from trace_waits.sql (continued)

```
    7    file 2     block 112
    6    file 7     block 5122
$
```

The meaning of the wait parameters for each type of wait event is visible in V$EVENT_NAME and is documented in an appendix to the *Oracle8i Reference* guide. However, this is a particularly weak section of the Oracle documentation. Much of the information is enigmatic, out-of-date, or inaccurate. Because the wait parameters are so vital to advanced performance tuning, this book explains the meaning of the wait parameters for each wait event discussed.

Reference

This section contains a quick reference to the parameters, events, statistics, and APT scripts mentioned in Chapter 2.

Parameters

Parameter	Description
_USE_VECTOR_POSTS	Vector posts enable multiple waiting processes to be posted in a single semaphore operation.
POST_WAIT_DEVICE	The post-wait driver is a pseudo device driver. Its functions are invoked when operations are performed against a device special file of that device type. Where this parameter is used, it specifies the path to the device file for the post-wait driver.
TIMED_STATISTICS	Should be set to TRUE whenever timing information may be required for tuning purposes, which is always.
USE_POST_WAIT_DRIVER	If this parameter exists, it should be set to TRUE in order to use the post-wait driver, instead of regular semaphore operations.

Events

Event	Description
10046	This is the event used to implement the DBMS_SUPPORT trace, which is a superset of Oracle's SQL_TRACE facility. At level 4, bind calls are included in the trace output; at level 8, wait events are included, which is the default level for DBMS_SUPPORT; and at level 12, both binds and waits are included. See the excellent Oracle Note 39817.1 for a detailed explanation of the raPw information in the trace file.

Statistics

Statistic	Source	Description
total_waits	V$SYSTEM_EVENT V$SESSION_EVENT	The number of distinct waits.
total_timeouts	V$SYSTEM_EVENT V$SESSION_EVENT	The number of waits that timed out instead of being posted.
logical_waits	*total_waits – total_timeouts*	A logical wait is a series of distinct waits for the same event. Each component wait times out, except the last, which is posted.
time_waited	V$SYSTEM_EVENT V$SESSION_EVENT	The total time waited.
average_wait	V$SYSTEM_EVENT V$SESSION_EVENT	The average time for each distinct wait.
average_logical	*time_waited / logical_waits*	The average time for each logical wait.
max_wait	V$SESSION_EVENT	The longest component wait by the session for the event.

APT Scripts

Script	Description
resource_waiters.sql	Shows which sessions have waited for a particular resource type, and for how long.
resource_waits.sql	Shows all the resources waited for, and the total waiting time, over the life of the instance, in order of severity.
routine_waits.sql	Reports the average time waited for each routine wait.
session_times.sql	Shows how much time a particular session has used working or waiting, and what is has been waiting for.
trace_waits.sql	Enables the DBMS_SUPPORT trace (event 10046, level 8) for a period in the sessions most affected by a particular type of resource wait. Used to sample the wait parameters, in order to diagnose performance problems.

3

Latches

There are numerous data structures in Oracle's System Global Area (SGA) that need to be accessed concurrently by many different database processes. It is essential that only one process be able to modify any particular data structure at one time, and that the data structure cannot be modified while it is being inspected. Oracle makes sure this does not happen by protecting all SGA data structures with either locks or latches. (See Chapter 6, *Memory*, for a description of the contents of the SGA and other memory areas.)

Latches and Locks

Latches are the more restrictive mechanism, because they do not allow multiple processes to inspect the protected data structure at the same time—they provide for exclusive access only.* Locks allow for better concurrency, because they may be held in a shared mode when the data structure is simply being inspected.

Another significant difference between locks and latches is request queuing. Requests for locks are queued if necessary and serviced in order, whereas latches do not support request queuing. If a request to get a latch fails because the latch is busy, the process just continues to retry until it succeeds. So latch requests are not necessarily serviced in order.

Because a latch can only be held by one process at a time, and because there is no inherent concept of queuing, the latch data structure itself is

---

* This is a simplification. The *redo copy* latches can be shared, but this is hardware dependent.

very simple—essentially just a single location in memory representing the state of the latch. And because the latch data structure is so simple, the functions to get and release a latch have very little work to do. By contrast, the data structures for locks are much more sophisticated because of their support for queuing and concurrency. So the functions to get, convert, and release locks have correspondingly more work to do.

Of course, it is necessary for Oracle to ensure that only one process at a time can modify the latch and lock data structures themselves. For latches this is easy. Because each latch is just a single location in memory, Oracle is able to use the TEST AND SET, LOAD AND CLEAR, or COMPARE AND SWAP instructions of the underlying hardware's instruction set for its latch get operations. Because these are simple machine instructions that are guaranteed to be atomic, no other locking mechanism is needed. This simplicity makes latch gets very efficient.

Oracle's lock data structures, on the other hand, have several parts, and therefore cannot be modified atomically. For this reason, Oracle actually protects operations on locks with latches. The type of latch used varies depending on the type of lock. For example, the cache buffer locks are indirectly protected by the *cache buffers chains* latches, and the row cache enqueue locks are protected by the *row cache objects* latch.

Because latches are efficient, Oracle often uses a latch, rather than a lock and latch combination, to protect data structures that are expected to be accessed only briefly and intermittently.

Parent and Child Latches

Most internal Oracle data structures that are protected by latches are protected by only one latch. However, in some cases more than one latch may be used. For example, there may be a number of *library cache* latches protecting different groups of objects in the library cache, and separate *cache buffers chains* latches are used to protect each of the database buffer cache hash chains.

Whenever a number of latches may be used to protect different parts of a structure, or different equivalent structures, these latches are called child latches. For each set of child latches of the same type there is one parent latch. In general, both the parent and child latches may be taken. In practice, however, the *library cache* parent latch is the only parent latch you are likely to see being taken, and even then this is a relatively rare occurrence by comparison with the activity against its child latches.

Somewhat confusingly, Oracle also refers to solitary latches that have no children as parent latches. So the V$LATCH_PARENT view contains one row for each of the solitary latches, as well as one row for each of the genuine parent latches. V$LATCH_CHILDREN has a row for each child latch. Thus, the union of these two views represents all latches.

The types of latches used by Oracle, and whether they are solitary latches or parent and child sets, varies with different releases of Oracle and operating system ports. The APT script *latch_types.sql* can be used to see what latch types are in use in your database, whether they are parent and child sets, and if so, how many child latches there are. Example 3-1 shows an extract of the output of this script.

Example 3-1. Sample Output from latch_types.sql

```
SQL> @latch_types

  TYPE TYPE                                         PARENT    CHILD
NUMBER NAME                                         LATCH   LATCHES
------ ------------------------------------------   ------  -------
     0 latch wait list                                   1        1
     1 process allocation                                1
     2 session allocation                                1
     3 session switching                                 1
     4 session idle bit                                  1        1
 . . .
```

APT Scripts and X$ Tables

A number of the APT scripts referred to in this book, like *latch_types.sql*, are based directly on the X$ tables, rather than the V$ views. This is often necessary because the V$ views do not contain the required information, or because querying the V$ views would impose an unsatisfactory load on the instance.

Because the X$ tables are only visible to the SYS schema, and because it would be bad practice to do anything as SYS unnecessarily, APT requires that you create a set of views that expose the X$ tables to other DBA schemata. This can be done with the *create_xviews.sql* script, which of course *must* be run as SYS. Unless these views exist, all APT scripts that are dependent on the X$ tables will fail.

Note that the X$ tables change from release to release, and so these APT scripts are often release specific. Make sure that you use the right scripts for your release of Oracle.

The V$LATCH view contains summary latch statistics grouped by latch type. V$LATCH should be your first point of reference when investigating a suspected latching problem. If the problem relates to a set of latches of the same type, you should consult V$LATCH_CHILDREN to investigate whether the distribution of activity across the child latches is even, and possibly V$LATCH_PARENT also to determine whether there has been any activity against the parent latch.

Latch Gets

When an Oracle process needs to access a data structure protected by a latch, it can request to get the latch in one of two modes—willing-to-wait mode or no-wait mode (also called immediate mode).

Willing-to-Wait Mode

Oracle expects latches to be held briefly and intermittently. So if a process attempts to get a latch in willing-to-wait mode and finds that the latch is not available, it will spin briefly and then try again. When a process spins, it executes a simple series of instructions a number of times, as a way of waiting before trying again. This is sometimes called an active wait because from the operating system's perspective, the process is still actively consuming CPU cycles, although it is really just waiting a while.

The amount of CPU time that a process will burn before trying to get the latch once again is very small and fixed (although it was tunable in Oracle7 using the _LATCH_SPIN_COUNT parameter). If the next attempt to get the latch fails again, the procedure will be repeated up to the number of times specified by the _SPIN_COUNT parameter. This parameter normally defaults to 2000 iterations in multi-processor environments.

Why spin?

The idea of spinning is that another process executing on another CPU may release the latch, thereby allowing the spinning process to proceed. Of course, it makes no sense to spin on a machine with just one CPU, and so Oracle does not.

The alternative to spinning is to relinquish the CPU and allow another process to use it. At first glance, this may seem like a good idea. However, for a CPU to stop executing one process and begin executing another, it must perform a context switch. That is, it must save the context of the first process, determine which process to schedule next, and then resume the context of the next process. The context of a process is essentially a set of CPU register values that describes the exact state of the process.

The implementation of context switches is highly machine dependent. In fact, it is typically written in assembly language. System vendors make every effort to minimize the size of the context data and optimize context switching by using tricks such as remapping memory addresses rather than copying data. Nevertheless, context switching remains an expensive operation because various kernel data structures have to be searched and updated. Access to these structures is protected by spinlocks, which are the equivalent of latches for the operating system. On a large and busy system, context switching normally consumes between 1% and 3% of CPU time. So if a context switch can be avoided by spinning briefly, then some CPU time can be saved, and the waiting time to obtain the latch can be minimized. For this reason, spinning briefly is normally preferable to relinquishing the CPU immediately.

Understanding the spin statistics

The latch statistics in the V$LATCH family of views record a *get* whenever a process acquires a latch in willing-to-wait mode. If the process fails to get the latch without spinning, a *miss* is recorded. If the latch is obtained after one or more spin iterations, a *spin get* is recorded. If the latch cannot be obtained while spinning, the process relinquishes the CPU and enters a sleep. No matter how many times the process subsequently wakes up, spins, and sleeps again, no further *gets* or *misses* will be recorded, and neither will a *spin get* be recorded if the latch is finally obtained while spinning. So, the number of times that a latch was obtained without spinning at all is *gets* − *misses*. I call these *simple gets*. The APT script *latch_gets.sql* shows the breakdown of gets into *simple gets*, *spin gets*, and gets that slept, called *sleep gets*. Example 3-2 shows some sample output.

Example 3-2. Sample Output from latch_gets.sql

```
SQL> @latch_gets

LATCH TYPE                      SIMPLE GETS        SPIN GETS        SLEEP GETS
------------------------------  -----------------  --------------   --------------
archive control                       228 100.00%      0  0.00%          0  0.00%
cache buffer handles                67399 100.00%      0  0.00%          0  0.00%
cache buffers chains           2940282897 100.00%  11811  0.00%      35999  0.00%
cache buffers lru chain          56863812  99.60%  44364  0.08%     182480  0.32%
dml lock allocation               2047579  99.99%     36  0.00%        199  0.01%
enqueue hash chains              14960087  99.95%   1139  0.01%       6603  0.04%
enqueues                         24759299 100.00%    165  0.00%        861  0.00%
...
```

Perhaps more interestingly, the APT script *latch_spins.sql* shows the effectiveness of spinning for each latch type, as illustrated in Example 3-3.

Example 3-3. Sample Output from latch_spins.sql

```
SQL> @latch_spins
```

LATCH TYPE	SPIN GETS	SLEEP GETS	SPIN HIT RATE
cache buffers lru chain	44752	182595	19.68%
redo allocation	29218	66781	30.44%
library cache	18997	43535	30.38%
cache buffers chains	11812	36001	24.70%
redo copy	606	18245	3.21%
messages	3968	8315	32.30%
enqueue hash chains	1139	6603	14.71%
system commit number	2312	5548	29.41%
undo global data	252	1327	15.96%
session idle bit	256	1198	17.61%
enqueues	165	861	16.08%
transaction allocation	80	535	13.01%
list of block allocation	47	353	11.75%
shared pool	272	295	47.97%
dml lock allocation	36	199	15.32%
global tx hash mapping	36	184	16.36%
latch wait list	27	95	22.13%
session allocation	13	78	14.29%
row cache objects	89	76	53.94%
ALL LATCHES	114080	372833	23.43%

Tuning the spin count

Clearly, increasing the _SPIN_COUNT parameter has the potential to improve the effectiveness of spinning, at the cost of using more CPU time on unsuccessful spins. Alternately, if many spins are unsuccessful, reducing the spin count will reduce the amount of CPU time spent spinning. In general, tuning the spin count is a matter of balancing the CPU time used spinning against the CPU time and elapsed time saved by avoiding context switches. A workable rule of thumb is to attempt to minimize the value of the following:

_SPIN_COUNT * *sleeps / misses*

which serves as an approximation of the cost of spinning. If in doubt, err in favor of a higher spin count rather than a lower one. In database instances with mild latching problems, it may be beneficial to increase the _SPIN_COUNT parameter significantly from its default value. This is particularly true if the number of active processes is of the same order of magnitude as the number of CPUs. In instances experiencing severe latch contention the optimum spin count is normally much less than the default, but more than one.

The API script *tune_spin_count.sql* can be used to try out alternate values for the _SPIN_COUNT parameter. It notes the spin statistics, then uses the ALTER SYSTEM SET "_SPIN_COUNT" command to change the spin count. After waiting for the specified period, it checks the spin statistics again and computes the effect of the new spin count over the interval. A sample dialog from this script is shown in Example 3-4. Be warned that no allowance is made for variations in load, so some variability in results is to be expected. Note also that trying a very high value for _SPIN_COUNT could upset your users!

Example 3-4. Sample Dialog from tune_spin_count.sql

```
SQL> @tune_spin_count

SPIN_COUNT
----------
2000

SPIN HIT RATE   SPIN COST
-------------   ----------
       93.53%           6

Enter new _spin_count value to try: 4000
Enter time to wait (in seconds): 900

SPIN HIT RATE   SPIN COST
-------------   ----------
       96.27%           4

SQL>
```

Of course, tuning the spin count should be the very last thing you do in response to latch contention. You should first identify which latches are subject to contention, and then attempt to understand why. You should then make every possible effort to prevent the contention. Only when you have completely run out of ideas should you attempt to minimize the effect of the contention by tuning the spin count.

Sleeps

If a willing-to-wait request fails, then before the process goes to sleep, it must arrange for itself to be woken up again. As described in Chapter 2, there are two mechanisms for a process that is sleeping to be woken up again. The normal mechanism for latch sleeps is a simple timeout. A process sleeping for a latch waits on its semaphore, but before it does so, it sets an alarm that will cause it to be signaled by the operating system at the end of a specified interval. The interval specified is variable. Initially the process will sleep for just one centisecond. If after waking up, the process again fails to obtain the latch, then the length of the second and any subsequent sleeps will be doubled under what is called the exponential backoff algorithm. The maximum sleep under the exponential backoff algorithm is set by the _MAX_EXPONENTIAL_SLEEP parameter, which defaults to 2 seconds in Oracle8. However, if the process is already holding other latches, then the maximum sleep time is reduced to the value of the _ MAX_SLEEP_HOLDING_LATCH parameter, which defaults to 4 centiseconds, and possibly further, in proportion with the number of other latches already being held.

Another task that the process performs before it goes to sleep is to update the session wait information visible in the V$SESSION_WAIT view to indicate that the process is waiting on a *latch free* wait. The wait parameters are shown in Table 3-1.

Table 3-1. Wait Parameters (latch free waits)

Parameter	Description
p1	The SGA address of the latch required; corresponds to the ADDR column of the V$LATCH_PARENT and V$LATCH_CHILDREN views (but *not* V$LATCH itself)
p2	The type of the latch; corresponds to the LATCH# column of the V$LATCH family of views
p3	The number of times that the process has slept during this attempt to acquire the latch

When the process wakes up again, it will update the session wait information to indicate that the wait is over, and if timed statistics are enabled, it will record the time for which it slept. The cumulative statistics for *latch free* waits that are visible in the V$SESSION_EVENT and V$SYSTEM_ EVENT views are also updated at this time. Note that consecutive sleeps during a single attempt to acquire a latch are recorded as separate waits. However, the latching statistics visible in the V$LATCH family of views are only updated once the latch has been acquired.

If a process fails to obtain a latch in either willing-to-wait or no-wait mode, then it updates the latch miss statistics which are visible in the V$LATCH_ MISSES view. This update is not protected by a latch, and so these statistics may not tally with those in V$LATCH. Each row in V$LATCH_MISSES represents a location in the Oracle server code from which a latch may be held. The NWFAIL_COUNT and SLEEP_COUNT columns record the number of no-wait get failures and sleeps, respectively, that occurred while the latch was being held from that particular location in the code. Unfortunately, considerable familiarity with the Oracle server code is required to be able to interpret the significance of these statistics. For what it's worth, the APT script *latch_where.sql* shows the distribution of sleeps against code locations.

Latch Wait Posting

The second mechanism whereby a process sleeping on a latch may be woken up is called *latch wait posting*. In this case, the next process to free the required latch will wake up the sleeping process. The waiting process must request latch wait posting before it goes to sleep. It does this by putting itself on a list of processes waiting to be posted, known as the latch wait list. When a process frees a latch, it checks the latch wait list, and if there is a process waiting for that latch, it posts the semaphore of the waiting process, which acts as a signal to the operating system to schedule the waiting process to run.

The benefit of latch wait posting is that there is a high probability of the waiting process obtaining the latch almost as soon as the latch is freed. Of course, there is also a significant cost to latch wait posting, namely maintaining the latch wait list data structure. This data structure is implemented as a set of singly linked lists through the process table in the SGA (visible as X$KSUPR.KSLLALAQ). Of course, as with any other data structure, the lists have to be protected by latches. Where latch wait posting is used extensively, the latch wait lists can become relatively long, with the result that the *latch wait list* latches are held longer and more frequently than otherwise. Indeed, it is not uncommon to see secondary contention on one of the *latch wait list* latches, when there is severe contention for some other latch for which latch wait posting is enabled.

By default, latch wait posting is enabled only for the *library cache* and *shared pool* latches. It can be disabled entirely by setting the _LATCH_WAIT_POSTING parameter to 0 (the default is 1), or it can be enabled for all latches by setting the parameter to 2. Changes to latch wait posting need to be carefully benchmarked. Disabling latch wait posting can be beneficial where contention on the *library cache* latch is severe, and enabling it for all latches can improve performance in cases of moderate contention for other latches. Even when enabled for all latches, latch wait posting will not always be requested for sleeps on the *cache buffers chains* latches.

The WAITERS_WOKEN column in the V$LATCH family of views shows the number of times that a waiter has been woken via the latch wait posting mechanism. This statistic can actually be greater than the number of misses, because it is possible for a process to be posted and yet fail to obtain the latch because some other process has taken it in the interim.

Latch Contention

We have already observed that Oracle expects latches to be held only briefly and intermittently. If the use of any latch is either not brief, or not intermittent, then contention for that latch is likely. An episode of latch contention begins when the latch is being held by one process and is required by two or more other processes. Until the backlog of demand is cleared, waiting processes must contend for the latch. This results in CPU time being ineffectively used, and in the extreme can have a disastrous effect on performance.

The severity of contention for a particular latch may be characterized in terms of the frequency, duration, and intensity of latch contention episodes. This can be assessed using the histogram of sleep counts contained in the SLEEP1 to SLEEP4 columns of V$LATCH. Note that no statistics are kept for sleep cycles longer than four iterations—the columns SLEEP5 to SLEEP11 are retained for compatibility with releases of Oracle prior to 7.3.

The histogram of sleep counts can also be used to determine the effectiveness (or otherwise) of attempts to reduce contention for the latch. However, the ratio of *sleeps* to *gets* serves as a better indicator of the effectiveness of latch tuning, because it accounts for simple gets as well as misses. I call this ratio, expressed as a percentage, the *sleep rate*. The sleep rate is calculated by the APT script *latch_sleeps.sql*. See Example 3-5 for sample output.

Example 3-5. Sample Output from latch_sleeps.sql

```
SQL> @latch_sleeps

LATCH TYPE                    IMPACT SLEEP RATE WAITS HOLDING    LEVEL
--------------------------- --------- ---------- ---------------- -------
library cache                 11224      0.03%              256         5
cache buffers chains           1295      0.00%                0         1
redo allocation                 713      0.01%             9613         7
system commit number            373      0.00%               66         8
enqueue hash chains             221      0.00%                3         4
redo copy                       210     22.30%                0         6
shared pool                     166      0.01%             1434         7
```

Example 3-5. Sample Output from latch_sleeps.sql (continued)

```
cache buffers lru chain       146    0.01%    336    3
messages                      135    0.01%      0    8
session allocation            113    0.02%      0    5
row cache objects              96    0.00%      0    4
enqueues                       75    0.00%    624    5
latch wait list                48    0.08%      1    9
session idle bit               47    0.00%      0    1
undo global data               14    0.00%      0    5
multiblock read objects        13    0.00%      8    3
sequence cache                 11    0.00%      0    8
dml lock allocation            10    0.00%      0    3
transaction allocation         10    0.00%      0    8
list of block allocation        4    0.00%      0    3
modify parameter values         2    0.03%      0    0
process allocation              1    0.02%      0    0
```

Note that there is an important difference between the sleep rate and the impact of a particular type of latch on overall performance. For example, in Example 3-5 the sleep rate for the *redo copy* latches is high (as is normal). However, because there are very few willing-to-wait gets on these latches, the impact of these sleeps is not the highest. The impact shown is based on the number of sleeps. However, not all sleeps are equal because of the exponential backoff algorithm. So the number of sleeps per *sleep get* is used as an indicator of the average length of sleeps against each latch, and this is multiplied by the number of sleeps to estimate the impact.

Latch Levels

It is very common for an Oracle process to need to hold a number of latches concurrently. Therefore, there might be a possibility of latching deadlocks occurring—namely, one process holding latch A and another process holding latch B, and both processes spinning and waiting for the alternate latch. Oracle ensures that this cannot happen by ensuring that latches are always taken in a defined order, when more than one latch is required. To support this, every latch in Oracle has a level between 0 and 15, and a 2-byte bitmap is maintained for every process representing the levels of the latches that the process is currently holding. When a process attempts to get a latch in willing-to-wait mode, a check is made to ensure that it is not already holding a latch at the same level or at a higher level. In general, if this rule is broken, an ORA-600 [504] internal error is raised.*

---

* However, this latch level rule is sometimes relaxed to allow two library cache child latches to be held simultaneously.

Contention for a high-level latch such as the *redo allocation* latch (level 6) can easily exacerbate contention for lower-level latches such as the *cache buffers chains* latches (level 1 in Oracle 8.1). This happens because processes needing the higher-level latch have to sleep while holding a lower-level latch. So the lower-level latches are held for much longer than normal. An indication of this factor is available in the WAITS_HOLDING_ LATCH column of the V$LATCH family of views. That statistic represents the number of times that a process missed on this latch while holding another latch. For example, the WAITS_HOLDING_LATCH statistic for the *redo allocation* latch counts both *spin gets* and *sleep gets* against the *redo allocation* latch while holding another latch such as a *cache buffers chains* latch.

No-Wait Mode

No-wait mode is used when Oracle is already holding one latch and needs to acquire another latch at the same level or at a lower level. A willing-to-wait request cannot be used in this case because of the dead-lock prevention requirement. In this case, Oracle can request the latch in no-wait mode, as long as no more than one pair of latches would be held at the same level. If the no-wait request succeeds, there is no risk of dead-lock and so all is well. However, if the request fails, there would be a risk of deadlock were the process to persist in its attempt to acquire the latch. Instead, the process releases all the higher-level latches that it holds, yields the CPU, and then immediately attempts to acquire them again in the correct order of level.

The *redo copy* latches are a slightly special case. No-wait mode is used for most gets against these latches, because Oracle can use any one of them to protect the copy into the log buffer. If the request for one copy latch fails, Oracle can perform the copy on another latch instead. Willing-to-wait mode is only used to get the last copy latch if no-wait gets against all the other copy latches have failed. This is normally a symptom of waits while holding the copy latches, such as contention for a higher-level latch, and so increasing the number of copy latches with the _LOG_ SIMULTANEOUS_COPIES parameter does not normally help.

Other than the *redo copy* latches, there are only a few types of latches that Oracle sometimes attempts to get in no-wait mode. For all other types of latches, the IMMEDIATE_GETS and IMMEDIATE_MISSES columns in the V$LATCH family of views are always zero.

From a performance point of view, immediate misses are not necessarily a problem. If the relinquished latches are reclaimed cheaply after the willing-to-wait get is satisfied, then the cost of the immediate miss is not inordinate. However, if there is a degree of contention for those other latches, then immediate misses exacerbate the problem by increasing the workload on those latches. Therefore, when tuning any latch you should attempt to eliminate immediate misses as well as sleeps. However, don't lose too much sleep over immediate misses unless you are sleeping too much on higher-level latches.

Latch Cleanups

It is a fact of life that Oracle processes sometimes die unexpectedly, and can die when holding a latch. It is the task of the Oracle PMON process to detect the unexpected death of user processes and perform cleanup actions. Among the cleanup actions that PMON performs first is latch cleanup. Latch cleanup is completed for all newly deceased processes, before any work is begun to roll back uncommitted transactions.

Latch cleanup is not merely a matter of freeing the latch. Latches are taken to manipulate data structures, and if a process dies holding a latch, there is every chance that the data structure protected by the latch may have been left in an inconsistent state. To support latch recovery, processes holding a latch in order to manipulate a structure write a record of their intended operation into the latch recovery area for that latch, prior to performing the operation. PMON's task is not just to free the latch, but first to recover the protected data structure. A latch is said to be in flux if latch recovery is necessary or in progress.

However, because PMON normally wakes up only every 3 seconds, Oracle has another way of initiating latch cleanup. If a process has repeatedly failed to acquire a latch, it will perform a latch activity test to check whether latch cleanup may be necessary. If there is no activity on the latch for 5 centiseconds, the process will post PMON, and PMON will check whether the process holding the latch has died and needs to be cleaned up.

When a process is performing a latch activity test, or waiting for PMON to check the process holding the latch, the V$SESSION_WAIT view shows that the process is waiting on a *latch activity* wait. The wait parameters are as shown in Table 3-2.

If latch contention is accompanied by numerous latch activity waits, the cause of both symptoms could be an operating system scheduling

Table 3-2. Wait Parameters (latch activity waits)

Parameter	Description
p1	The SGA address of the latch required.
p2	The type of the latch.
p3	0 for the latch activity test. Otherwise, the process number of the possibly deceased latch holder being checked by PMON.

problem that is preventing the latch holder from releasing the latch quickly enough.

DLM Latches

Instance locks are used for inter-instance locking and communication between the instances of an Oracle parallel server database. A separate part of the SGA contains the structures needed for instance locks. A set of latches is used to protect these structures. In release 8.0, the latching statistics for these latches were reported separately in V$DLM_LATCH. From release 8.1, the Distributed Lock Manager (DLM) latching statistics have been merged into V$LATCH.

LMON performs latch cleanup for DLM latches in cooperation with PMON.

Advanced Latching Control

Some operating systems support a facility called multi-processing control. This enables an authorized user process to influence its CPU scheduling in a variety of ways. Where available, Oracle can use certain multi-processing control features. The following features affect the latching mechanism.

Preemption Control

Preemption control enables Oracle to suspend the operation of the normal operating system process preemption mechanism during performance-critical operations—in particular, when holding a latch. This means that the Oracle process can continue to run on its CPU until it explicitly enables preemption again, or until it blocks on an operating system event such as an I/O request, semaphore operation, or page fault. The process will not be pre-empted at the end of its time-slice by a higher priority process of the time-sharing priority class. This means that operations protected by latches complete as quickly as possible, and so the risk of latch contention is greatly reduced. If preemption control is available to Oracle, it is used by default unless disabled using the _NO_PREEMPT parameter.

CPU Yielding

CPU yielding enables Oracle processes to offer to yield the CPU during a spin. If there is another runnable process of higher priority able to use the CPU, that process is scheduled, and the yielding process is placed at the end of its run queue, but it remains runnable. Otherwise, if there are no other higher-priority processes able to use the CPU, then the process will continue to spin for its latch. The frequency with which Oracle will offer to yield the CPU while spinning is controlled by the _SPIN_YIELD_CPU_ FREQ parameter, which defaults to the default value of the _SPIN_COUNT parameter. If CPU yielding is available, and if these two parameters have the same value, the effect is that the process will begin a new spin without sleeping if there is no other process available to use the CPU. Thus, CPU yielding enables Oracle processes to obtain latches as quickly as possible without consuming otherwise usable CPU time.

Affinity Control

Affinity control enables Oracle processes to disable and re-enable the normal operating system affinity mechanism which attempts to weakly bind a process to the last CPU it ran on. If a process runs on the same CPU as before, many of the memory address and value pairs (cache lines) required for its execution may still be available in that CPU's cache. This can result in greatly reduced memory access by that CPU, and thus much faster execution. However, faster execution is not necessary when all the process is doing is spinning for a latch, and faster execution is less important than earlier execution when the process has been sleeping holding a latch that other processes may need. Where it is available, Oracle uses affinity control to optimize latching automatically. Incidentally, it is not recommended to use explicit processor binding for Oracle processes. Otherwise, runnable processes will not be migrated to idle CPUs.

Oracle can use multi-processing control features to improve the performance of large, highly active instances significantly, and the biggest impact is in the area of latching. However, under many operating systems some or all of these features are not available, or are not available to the processes of ordinary users such as "oracle." Where these features are available, the "oracle" user must be specifically authorized to use them. In some cases, such authorizations are not persistent, and so the authorization commands must be placed in the system startup scripts to ensure that Oracle will always be able to use these features. Check your operating system documentation for an *mpctl()* system call and related entries to

determine whether your operating system supports multi-processing
control features for ordinary user processes, and if so, how to enable them.

Reference

This section contains a quick reference to the parameters, statistics, waits,
and APT scripts mentioned in Chapter 3.

Parameters

Parameter	Description
_LATCH_WAIT_POSTING	Latch wait posting is a mechanism whereby a process can be woken (posted) when the latch that it requires becomes available. If this parameter is set to 0, latch wait posting is disabled. If this parameter is set to 1 (the default), latch wait posting is enabled for library cache, library cache load lock, and shared pool latches only. Any other setting results in latch wait posting being enabled for all latches.
_MAX_EXPONENTIAL_ SLEEP	Consecutive sleeps during a single attempt to acquire a latch become progressively longer, under an exponential backoff algorithm, up to the limit specified by this parameter. Defaults to 200 centiseconds in Oracle8.
_MAX_SLEEP_HOLDING_ LATCH	The maximum sleep allowed under the exponential backoff algorithm when the sleeping process is holding another latch. Defaults to 4 centiseconds.
_NO_PREEMPT	If this parameter is set to TRUE (the default) Oracle will use the operating system's preemption control mechanism, if available, to minimize the risk of processes sleeping while holding a latch.
_SPIN_COUNT	The number of iterations to perform before sleeping when spinning to acquire a latch. Defaults to 1 on single CPU systems, and 2000 on most multi-processor machines.
_SPIN_YIELD_CPU_FREQ	This parameter controls the frequency with which an Oracle process will offer to yield the CPU if possible during a spin. If a higher-priority process is runnable, it will be scheduled, and the yielding process will be placed at the end of the run queue without sleeping. Defaults to the default value of _SPIN_COUNT. If _SPIN_COUNT is tuned, this parameter should normally be tuned as well.

Statistics

Statistic	Source	Description
immediate gets	V$LATCH family	Successful latch get requests in no-wait mode
immediate misses	V$LATCH family	Latch get requests in no-wait mode that failed
gets	V$LATCH family	Completed willing-to-wait latch acquisitions
misses	V$LATCH family	Gets that waited because the latch was in use
simple gets	*gets - misses*	Gets completed without waiting at all
spin gets	V$LATCH family	Gets that obtained the latch by spinning, but did not sleep
sleep gets	*misses - spin gets*	Gets that required one or more sleeps
spin get rate	*100 * spin gets / misses*	A measure of the effectiveness of spinning
spin cost	*_SPIN_COUNT * sleeps / misses*	A measure of the cost of spinning
sleeps	V$LATCH family	Total number of times that processes slept while waiting for the latch
sleep1	V$LATCH family	Gets that slept once
sleep2	V$LATCH family	Gets that slept twice
sleep3	V$LATCH family	Gets that slept three times
sleep4	V$LATCH family	Gets that slept four times
sleep rate	*100 * sleeps / gets*	A measure of the severity of contention for the latch
sleep impact	*sleeps^2 / sleep gets*	An estimate of the relative impact of latch sleeps on overall performance
waiters woken	V$LATCH family	The number of times that waiters were posted due to latch wait posting
waits holding latch	V$LATCH family	The number of misses while holding another latch

Waits

Event	Description
latch activity	A process that has repeatedly failed to acquire a latch will perform a latch activity test to check whether latch cleanup may be necessary. This wait occurs both during the activity test and while waiting for latch cleanup if necessary.
latch free	Latch free waits are just sleeps by another name.
wait for DLM latch	This wait corresponds to latch free waits, but for DLM latches.
wait for influx DLM latch	The DLM latch needed latch recovery.

APT Scripts

Script	Description
create_xviews.sql	Some APT scripts are based on the X$ tables. Before those scripts can be used, this script must be run as SYS to create the required views on the X$ tables.
latch_gets.sql	Shows the breakdown of willing-to-wait gets into simple gets, spin gets, and sleep gets.
latch_levels.sql	Like *latch_types.sql*, but shows the level for each latch type.
latch_sleeps.sql	Shows the sleep rate and impact for latch sleeps. Used to determine the priority of latch tuning issues.
latch_spins.sql	Shows the number of spin gets and sleep gets and calculates the spin hit rate for each latch and for all latches.
latch_types.sql	Shows all latch types ordered by number, whether they are solitary latches or parent/child sets, and how many children there are. For elegance and performance, this script is based directly on X$KSLLT.
latch_where.sql	Shows where in the Oracle server code latch gets have been failing. This code is based directly on the X$ tables in order to access a column not projected by the V$LATCH_MISSES view.
tune_spin_count.sql	Used to alter the spin count and then monitor spin statistics for an interval to determine whether there has been an improvement.

4

Locks

Oracle uses latches to protect data structures that are accessed briefly and intermittently. However, latches are not suitable for protecting resources that may be needed for a relatively long time, such as database tables. In such cases, a lock must be used instead. Locks allow sessions to join a queue for a resource that is not immediately available. This avoids spinning. Locks also allow multiple sessions to share a resource if their activities are compatible.

Lock Usage

Oracle uses locks for many different purposes. The following are the most important ones to understand for performance tuning.

Transaction Locks and Row-Level Locks

Oracle's much vaunted row-level locks are subtle. When a transaction modifies a row, its transaction identifier is recorded in an entry in the interested transaction list (ITL) in the header of the data block itself, and the row header is modified to point to that ITL entry. Once these changes have been made, no lock is retained. The ITL entry for the uncommitted transaction, together with the row header that references it, constitutes an implicit lock on the row.

When another transaction wants to modify the same row, and sees that an uncommitted transaction has modified that row, that transaction waits, not on a row-level lock, but on the transaction lock for the blocking transaction.

When the blocking transaction commits or rolls back, its transaction lock will be released. Its implicit row-level locks are thereby released, and so the blocked transaction can then proceed. Note that rolling back to a save-point does not free previously blocked transactions that were waiting for a row-level lock.

Buffer Locks

Row-level locks protect data integrity at the lowest feasible level of granularity, and remain in force for the duration of a transaction. However, Oracle also needs short-term block-level locks to be in force while accessing or modifying blocks in its cache.

Buffer locks are used to provide simple read/write locking for blocks in the database buffer cache. Although they are often taken for granted and seldom mentioned, buffer locks are essential to data integrity, and can feature prominently in certain performance tuning scenarios.

Data Dictionary Locks

The definitions of database objects in the data dictionary must be protected while they are being referenced. This is necessary to prevent those objects from being dropped, and to prevent their definitions from being changed, while they are being used. Dictionary locks must be held while dependent SQL statements are being parsed or executed, and must be retained for the duration of dependent transactions.

Several types of locks are used for dictionary locking. All of these are covered in some detail later in this chapter. The data dictionary rows themselves are locked with row cache enqueue locks. Dependent SQL statements are protected with library cache pins, and dependent transactions hold DML (Data Manipulation Language) locks. Logically, both DML locks and library cache pins are dependent on the corresponding row cache enqueue locks. However, this dependency is implicit in the code, rather than explicit in the structures.

Lock Modes

Locks are applied to both compound and simple objects. The classic example of a compound object and its component parts is a table and its rows. A cache buffer is an example of a simple object. Simple objects may only be locked in the following modes:

Exclusive

If a session needs to modify a simple object, then an exclusive lock is required on the resource to prevent any concurrent access.

Shared

If a session needs to inspect a simple object, then a shared lock on the resource is sufficient to ensure that the data structure will not be modified by another session, while allowing concurrent shared access.

Null

If a session has some information cached about an object, then a null mode lock may be held as a placeholder, even when the resource is not actively being used. A null mode lock does not inhibit any concurrent access, but if the resource is invalidated, the null mode lock acts as a trigger for the session to invalidate its private cached information. There is an important difference between holding a null mode lock, and not holding a lock at all.

In addition to the modes above, compound objects may also be locked in the following modes:

Sub-shared

If a session needs shared access to part of a compound object, then a shared lock on the entire compound resource would be unduly restrictive, because it would prevent exclusive access to other parts of the compound resource. In such cases, a sub-shared lock is used instead.

Sub-exclusive

If a session needs exclusive access to part of a compound resource, then a sub-exclusive lock is sufficiently restrictive.

Shared-sub-exclusive

This lock mode is used when a session needs exclusive access to part of a compound resource and shared access to the entire compound resource at the same time.

These lock modes apply both to local locks and to the instance locks that are used between parallel server instances. However, different terminology is used for instance locks. Table 4-1 shows the corresponding lock mode names together with the symbolic and numeric representations used in dumps and wait parameter values.

It is important to understand which lock modes are compatible with one another. Table 4-2 shows the complete lock mode compatibility matrix.

Table 4-1. Lock Modes

Local Lock Modes			Instance Lock Modes		
Name	Symbol	Number	Name	Symbol	Number
(No lock)	NLCK	0			
Null	N	1	Null	NL	0
Sub-Shared	SS	2	Concurrent Read	CR	1
Sub-Exclusive	SX	3	Concurrent Write	CW	2
Shared	S	4	Protected Read	PR	3
Shared-Sub-Exclusive	SSX	5	Protected Write	PW	4
Exclusive	X	6	Exclusive	EX	5

Table 4-2. Lock Mode Compatibility

	N	SS	SX	S	SSX	X
N	Yes	Yes	Yes	Yes	Yes	Yes
SS	Yes	Yes	Yes	Yes	Yes	No
SX	Yes	Yes	Yes	No	No	No
S	Yes	Yes	No	Yes	No	No
SSX	Yes	Yes	No	No	No	No
X	Yes	No	No	No	No	No

Enqueue Locks

Many of Oracle's locks are called *enqueue locks*. To enqueue a lock request is to place that request on the queue for its resource. So although the word "enqueue" is strictly speaking a verb, it is used adjectivally in the term *enqueue lock*. It is also used as a noun when referring to a particular enqueue resource, such as the CF (control file) enqueue.

Oracle uses two classes of local locks—those for which the lock and resource data structures are dynamically allocated in the shared pool, and those that use fixed arrays for the lock and resource data structures. Although almost all types of lock requests may be enqueued, the term *enqueue* should be taken to refer exclusively to those locks that use the fixed arrays for the lock and resource data structures, unless otherwise qualified.

Enqueue Resources

The fixed array for enqueue resources is sized by the ENQUEUE_ RESOURCES parameter. The number of slots in this array that are in use varies from time to time, and these can be seen in V$RESOURCE. Each row in V$RESOURCE represents a resource that is currently locked in any mode by one or more sessions. These resources are not persistent in that they are no longer defined once all locks on the resource have been released.

Rows in V$RESOURCE are identified by a two-character code representing the type of resource, and two numeric fields used to encode either the resource identity or the activities protected by locks on the resource, depending on the resource type. For example, resources of type TX represent entries in the transaction table of a rollback segment. The high-order two bytes of the first identifier contain the rollback segment number, and the low-order two bytes contain the transaction table slot number, while the second identifier contains the rollback segment wrap or sequence number.

All enqueue operations access the enqueue resource structure via a hash table. The hash value is based on the resource type and the numeric identifiers. The length of the enqueue hash table is set by the _ENQUEUE_HASH parameter. The default value of this parameter is derived directly from the PROCESSES parameter, as follows:

$$45 + 2 * (PROCESSES + \lfloor PROCESSES/10 \rfloor)$$

Because _ENQUEUE_HASH is derived directly from PROCESSES rather than from ENQUEUE_RESOURCES, it may be necessary to tune _ENQUEUE_HASH explicitly if ENQUEUE_RESOURCES has been raised significantly from its default value. Otherwise lengthy enqueue hash chains may develop. As with all hash tables, if you have cause to tune the number of buckets, you should make it a prime number (see the sidebar, "Hash Tables and Prime Numbers").

The enqueue hash chains are accessed under the protection of the *enqueue hash chains* latches. The number of child enqueue hash chains latches is set by the _ENQUEUE_HASH_CHAIN_LATCHES parameter, which defaults to the CPU_COUNT. In a high concurrency environment, sleeps may be recorded against the enqueue hash chains latches if the hash chains are allowed to become unduly long. However, sleeps against these latches should normally be regarded as a secondary result of contention for a higher-level latch, rather than attributed to long hash chains.

Enqueue Locking

In addition to the enqueue resources, a second fixed array is used for enqueue locking—namely, the enqueue locks themselves. The size of the

---

Hash Tables and Prime Numbers

Oracle uses hash tables internally so that objects can be located efficiently. For example, a hash table is used to locate database blocks in the buffer cache, and another hash table is used to locate named objects in the library cache.

To locate an object via a hash table, Oracle uses an algorithm to convert the object's name or identifier into a number. That number may be much larger than the size of the hash table, so it is converted to an index into the hash table using a simple modulus function.

Multiple objects may map to the same hash table entry. This is called a hash collision. Oracle normally resolves hash collisions using collision chains. This means that objects that map to the same hash table entry are linked together using a chain of pointers. These objects are said to fall into the same hash bucket.

The performance of hash-based access is sensitive to the length of the hash chains because they must be searched linearly. Therefore hash tables must be large enough to ensure that the average hash chain length remains short.

Long hash chains can also develop if the distribution of objects to hash buckets is uneven. This happens if there is any pattern in the names of the objects being hashed that the hash function is not able to randomize. This is surprisingly common.

By making the number of hash buckets a prime number, you can greatly reduce the risk of any pattern in the hash values resulting in hash collisions once the modulus function has been applied.

---

enqueue locks fixed array is set by the _ENQUEUE_LOCKS parameter, and the active rows can be seen in V$ENQUEUE_LOCK.

An enqueue lock structure is used by each session waiting for or holding a lock on a resource. If one or more sessions are waiting for locks on a resource, then their enqueue lock structures are linked together into a two-way linked list, with the enqueue resource structure as the list header. This linked list is maintained and serviced in the order in which the locks were requested. For example, if a lock is held in shared mode, and the first waiter requires access to the resource in exclusive mode, then other sessions that require shared access must queue for the resource behind the first waiter, despite the fact that their requests are compatible with the mode in which the resource is currently locked.

Similar two-way linked lists are used to link together the enqueue lock structures for sessions holding a lock on the resource, and for sessions waiting to change the mode of the lock that they are holding.

The operation of changing the mode of a lock is called an enqueue conversion. For example, if a transaction holds a lock on a particular table in sub-share mode, and needs to update a row of that table, then the enqueue lock must be converted to sub-exclusive mode. However, if the resource is currently locked in an incompatible mode by another session, then the conversion cannot proceed immediately and the enqueue lock structure is placed in the conversion queue. Enqueue conversions are serviced in order before new enqueue requests.

During enqueue operations, modifications to the enqueue resources and enqueue locks fixed array free lists (see the sidebar, "Fixed Array Free Lists") are made under the protection of the *enqueues* latch. There is only one enqueues latch, and it is often taken and released twice during the course of a single enqueue operation. However, the relevant enqueue hash chains latch is held for the duration of the operation.

Enqueue Waits

An enqueue wait occurs whenever an enqueue request or enqueue conversion cannot be granted immediately because another session is holding a lock on the resource in an incompatible mode. The blocked process records an *enqueue* wait. The wait parameters are shown in Table 4-3.

Table 4-3. Wait Parameters (enqueue waits)

Parameter	Description
p1	The high order 2 bytes contain the ASCII codes for the resource type. The low-order 2 bytes contain the mode in which a lock is required.
p2	The id1 identifier for the resource.
p3	The id2 identifier for the resource.

Whenever a session releases an enqueue lock, it examines the lock request and conversion queues for the resource and, if appropriate, posts the next process that will be able to acquire a lock on the resource.

Processes waiting in an enqueue wait also set an alarm before they begin to wait. The timeout duration is dependent on the type of resource. For most enqueues, the enqueue wait timeout is 3 seconds.

Consecutive waits during a single attempt to acquire an enqueue lock are recorded as separate waits in the session and system wait statistics.

However, the *enqueue waits* statistic in V$SYSSTAT is only incremented by one, after the lock has been acquired, as are the *enqueue requests* and *enqueue conversions* statistics. Note also that the *enqueue timeouts* statistic in V$SYSSTAT does not represent the number of enqueue wait timeouts. Rather, this statistic is incremented when an enqueue request or enqueue conversion is aborted entirely. This can be due to a distributed transaction timeout, but usually relates to locks requested in no-wait mode.

Fixed Array Free Lists

The free slots in each of Oracle's fixed arrays are maintained on a free list. For each of these arrays, there is a free list header pointer that points to one of the free slots in the array. That slot, in turn, holds a pointer to the next free slot in the free list, and so on.

Free slots are always taken from the head of the free list, and are always returned to the head of the free list. This means that the tail of the free list normally remains unused, and the high-water mark is only advanced when necessary. This fact was used by the APT script *fixed_table_hwms.sql* under Oracle7 to extract the maximum usage of each fixed array from the corresponding X$ tables. This script is redundant in Oracle8, because the same functionality is now provided by the V$RESOURCE_LIMIT view.

The free list for each fixed array must be protected by a latch. For example, the *process allocation* latch protects the free list for the array of processes, and the *session allocation* latch protects the free list for the array of sessions.

If V$SYSSTAT shows a significant number of enqueue waits, then a breakdown of the resource types for which these waits have been sustained can be obtained from X$KSQST, or from the APT script *enqueue_stats.sql*. Unfortunately, X$KSQST does not contains any indication of the duration of the waits, so care is needed when interpreting these figures.

It is sometimes suggested that ENQUEUE_RESOURCES should be increased to combat enqueue waits. But please note that there is absolutely no substance to this suggestion. Oracle will return an ORA-52 or ORA-53 error if it fails to find a free slot in the enqueue resources or enqueue locks fixed arrays respectively. Beyond that, the setting of the ENQUEUE_RESOURCES and _ENQUEUE_LOCKS parameters is unimportant.

The V$RESOURCE_LIMIT view should be used to adjust your settings for the ENQUEUE_RESOURCES and _ENQUEUE_LOCKS parameters to ensure that you will not run out of slots in these arrays. You can afford to be generous, because slots in these arrays only take on the order of 72 bytes and 60 bytes respectively. I like to maintain headroom of at least 20% above the maximum utilization ever recorded.

Deadlock Detection

Oracle performs automatic deadlock detection for enqueue locking deadlocks. Deadlock detection is initiated whenever an enqueue wait times out, if the resource type required is regarded as deadlock sensitive, and if the lock state for the resource has not changed. If any session that is holding a lock on the required resource in an incompatible mode is waiting directly or indirectly for a resource that is held by the current session in an incompatible mode, then a deadlock exists.

If a deadlock is detected, the session that was unlucky enough to find it aborts its lock request and rolls back its current statement in order to break the deadlock. Note that this is a rollback of the current statement only, not necessarily the entire transaction. Oracle places an implicit savepoint at the beginning of each statement, called the default savepoint, and it is to this savepoint that the transaction is rolled back in the first case. This is enough to resolve the technical deadlock. However, the interacting sessions may well remain blocked.

An ORA-60 error is returned to the session that found the deadlock, and if this exception is not handled, then depending on the rules of the application development tool, the entire transaction is normally rolled back, and a deadlock state dump written to the user dump destination directory. This, of course, resolves the deadlock entirely. The *enqueue deadlocks* statistic in V$SYSSTAT records the number of times that an enqueue deadlock has been detected.

Application developers can eliminate all risk of enqueue deadlocks by ensuring that transactions requiring multiple resources always lock them in the same order. However, in complex applications, this is easier said than done, particularly if an ad hoc query tool is used. To be safe, you should adopt a strict locking order, but you must also handle the ORA-60 exception appropriately. In some cases it may be sufficient to pause for three seconds, and then retry the statement. However, in general, it is safest to roll back the transaction entirely, before pausing and retrying.

Blocking Locks

Oracle resolves true enqueue deadlocks so quickly that overall system activity is scarcely affected. However, blocking locks can bring application processing to a standstill. For example, if a long-running transaction takes a shared mode lock on a key application table, then all updates to that table must wait.

There are numerous ways of attempting to diagnose blocking lock situations, normally with the intention of killing the offending session. I will mention just a few.

Blocking locks are almost always TX (transaction) locks or TM (table) locks. When a session waits on a TX lock, it is waiting for that transaction to either commit or roll back. The reason for waiting is that the transaction has modified a data block, and the waiting session needs to modify the same part of that block. In such cases, the row wait columns of V$SESSION can be useful in identifying the database object, file, and block numbers concerned, and even the row number in the case of row locks. V$LOCKED_OBJECT can then be used to obtain session information for the sessions holding DML locks on the crucial database object. This is based on the fact that sessions with blocking TX enqueue locks always hold a DML lock as well, unless DML locks have been disabled.

It may not be adequate, however, to identify a single blocking session, because it may, in turn, be blocked by another session. To address this requirement, Oracle's *utllockt.sql* script gives a tree-structured report showing the relationship between blocking and waiting sessions. Some DBAs are loath to use this script because it creates a temporary table, which will block if another space management transaction is caught behind the blocking lock. Although this is extremely unlikely, the same information can be obtained from the DBA_WAITERS view if necessary. The DBA_WAITERS view is created by Oracle's *catblock.sql* script.

Some application developers attempt to evade blocking locks by preceding all updates with a SELECT FOR UPDATE NOWAIT statement. However, if they allow user interaction between taking a sub-exclusive lock in this way and releasing it, then a more subtle blocking lock situation can still occur. If a user goes out to lunch while holding a sub-exclusive lock on a table, then any shared lock request on the whole table will block at the head of the request queue, and all other lock requests will queue behind it.

Diagnosing such situations and working out which session to kill is not easy, because the diagnosis depends on the order of the waiters. Most blocking lock detection utilities do not show the request order, and do not consider that a waiter can block other sessions even when it is not actually holding any locks. The APT script *enqueue_locks.sql* shows the locks held and wanted for each resource in order, together with the number of seconds that the lock has been held or wanted. This is intended to supplement other blocking lock detection utilities, such as Oracle's *utllockt.sql*.

Application developers can greatly reduce the risk of blocking lock problems by adopting an optimistic locking strategy (see the sidebar, "Optimistic Locking"), and by cultivating an aversion to coarse granularity locking and so designing their applications to run without DML locks.

Distributed Transactions

For distributed transactions, Oracle is unable to distinguish blocking locks and deadlocks, because not all of the lock information is available locally. To prevent distributed transaction deadlocks, Oracle times out any call in a distributed transaction if it has not received any response within the number of seconds specified by the _DISTRIBUTED_LOCK_TIMEOUT parameter. This timeout defaults to 60 seconds. If a distributed transaction times out, an ORA-2049 error is returned to the controlling session. Robust applications should handle this exception in the same way as local enqueue deadlocks.

Similarly, under release 8.0, parallel transactions, which consist of multiple sibling transaction branches, could deadlock undetectably with other simple transactions. If a simple transaction was blocked by one branch of a global transaction, and was blocking another, then Oracle's normal deadlock detection mechanism in release 8.0 would fail to detect the deadlock. To prevent this, Oracle timed out any enqueue lock acquisition or conversion request in a branch of a parallel transaction as though it were a distributed transaction, and an ORA-99 error was returned. The PARALLEL_ TRANSACTION_RESOURCE_TIMEOUT parameter, which defaulted to 300 seconds, was used to control this timeout. In release 8.1, the deadlock detection algorithm has been improved to detect these deadlocks, and so this timeout is no longer required.

ITL Entry Shortages

There is an interested transaction list (ITL) in the variable header of each Oracle data block. When a new block is formatted for a segment, the initial number of entries in the ITL is set by the INITRANS parameter for the segment. Free space permitting, the ITL can grow dynamically if

Optimistic Locking

Consider an airline seat reservation application. Two different customers may simultaneously ask two different operators whether a seat is available on a particular flight. What should the application do?

The application can use SELECT FOR UPDATE NOWAIT to retrieve the information. This guarantees that if a seat appears to be available, then it has already been locked, and a booking for that seat will be able to be successfully taken. This is called early locking, or *pessimistic locking*.

The alternative is to defer the taking of a lock until the customer resolves to make a booking. This is called late locking, or *optimistic locking*.

The choice of either pessimistic or optimistic locking affects the design of both business and application processes. So careful thought is needed. Pessimistic locking should be avoided where possible, despite being slightly easier to implement, because it increases the risk of blocking locks.

required, up to the limit imposed by the database block size, or the MAXTRANS parameter for the segment, whichever is less.

Every transaction that modifies a data block must record its transaction identifier and the rollback segment address for its changes to that block in an ITL entry. (However, for discrete transactions, there is no rollback segment address for the changes.) Oracle searches the ITL for a reusable or free entry. If all the entries in the ITL are occupied by uncommitted transactions, then a new entry will be dynamically created, if possible.

If the block does not have enough internal free space (24 bytes) to dynamically create an additional ITL entry, then the transaction must wait for a transaction using one of the existing ITL entries to either commit or roll back. The blocked transaction waits in shared mode on the TX enqueue for one of the existing transactions, chosen pseudo-randomly. The row wait columns in V$SESSION show the object, file, and block numbers of the target block. However, the ROW_WAIT_ROW# column remains unset, indicating that the transaction is not waiting on a row-level lock, but is probably waiting for a free ITL entry.

The most common cause of ITL entry shortages is a zero PCTFREE setting. Think twice before setting PCTFREE to zero on a segment that might be subject to multiple concurrent updates to a single block, even though those updates may not increase the total row length. The degree of concurrency that a block can support is dependent on the size of its ITL, and failing that, the amount of internal free space. Do not, however, let this warning scare you into using unnecessarily large INITRANS or PCTFREE settings. Large PCTFREE settings compromise data density and degrade table scan performance, and non-default INITRANS settings are seldom warranted.

One case in which a non-default INITRANS setting is warranted is for segments subject to parallel DML. If a child transaction of a PDML transaction encounters an ITL entry shortage, it will check whether the other ITL entries in the block are all occupied by its sibling transactions and, if so, the transaction will roll back with an ORA-12829 error, in order to avoid self-deadlock. The solution in this case is to be content with a lower degree of parallelism, or to rebuild the segment with a higher INITRANS setting. A higher INITRANS value is also needed if multiple serializable transactions may have concurrent interest in any one block.

Row Cache Enqueues

A cache of rows from the data dictionary is kept in the shared pool. This cache serves not only to reduce physical access to the data dictionary tables in the SYSTEM tablespace, but also enables fine-grained locking of individual data dictionary rows. The need for data dictionary locking was introduced at the start of this chapter (see "Data Dictionary Locks").

The locks on the data dictionary rows themselves are called row cache enqueue locks. These locks are implemented in much the same way as general enqueue locks. The cached data dictionary row acts as the resource structure, and enqueue lock structures are dynamically allocated from the shared pool as required. Locks can be requested, converted, and released, and requests can wait and time out, just like the general enqueue locks. However, row cache enqueue locks are not included in V$LOCK. In fact, they are not visible anywhere except in system and process state dumps.

Depending on the operation, some row cache enqueue locks are requested in no-wait mode and an ORA-54 error is returned if the lock is not immediately available. Otherwise, row cache lock requests are enqueued if necessary, and the process waits on a *row cache lock* wait. The parameters for this wait are shown in Table 4-4.

The numeric codes used for the lock modes in the parameters for this wait are those for instance locks, rather than local locks, even when running single-instance Oracle. However, this wait is relatively rare in single-instance

Table 4-4. Wait Parameters (row cache lock waits)

Parameter	Description
p1	A number corresponding to the CACHE# column of V$ROWCACHE representing the data dictionary table for which a row lock is needed
p2	The mode in which the lock is already held
p3	The mode in which the lock is needed

Oracle, resulting only from resource conflicts, whereas it is routine in parallel server because new lock requests must be socialized via the distributed lock manager.

Oracle does not expect row cache enqueue lock acquisitions and conversions to block for more than a few seconds. Therefore, *row cache lock* waits time out every 3 seconds, and if the lock has still not been acquired after 100 timeouts (5 minutes), an internal deadlock is assumed, and the operation is aborted. A message is written to the alert log saying that a process "WAITED TOO LONG FOR A ROW CACHE ENQUEUE LOCK," and a process state dump is written to a trace file. Except for DDL against a long-running, in-use function, procedure, or package, this error should be treated as an Oracle bug and reported to Oracle Support.

Library Cache Locks and Pins

The library cache is not one cache, but many. It contains the pseudo code for PL/SQL program units. It contains parse trees and execution plans for shareable SQL statements. It also contains abstract representations in a form called DIANA of the database objects referenced by the SQL statements. The information is needed in this form for PL/SQL program unit compilation and SQL statement parsing and execution, despite the fact that the dictionary cache contains the same information in a different form. The library cache also contains control structures such as synonym translations, dependency tracking information, and library cache locks and pins.

Library cache locks are referred to as breakable parse locks in the Oracle documentation. They are applied to the library cache objects for SQL statements and PL/SQL program units, and recursively to the library cache objects for the database objects on which they depend. Library cache locks are held in shared mode during parse operations and are converted to null mode thereafter. If a DDL statement later modifies the definition of a database object, then the library cache information for that database object and all dependent library cache objects is invalidated by breaking the library cache locks.

Library cache locks can only be broken, however, when the library cache object is not also pinned. A pin is applied to the library cache object for a PL/SQL program unit or SQL statement while it is being compiled, parsed, or executed. Pins are normally held in shared mode, but are also held in exclusive mode while the library cache information for the object is being changed. The library cache objects for pipes and sequences are most subject to change. When a library cache object is pinned, pins are applied to all referenced objects in turn. When a pin is applied to the library cache object for a database object, then a corresponding row cache enqueue lock is acquired on the underlying data dictionary row, thereby preventing conflicting DDL.

Every object in the library cache has a handle that acts as the resource structure for library cache locks and pins. The handle, lock, and pin structures are all dynamically allocated within the shared pool. The handle implements two-way linked lists of locks held, locks waited for, pins held, and pins waited for. Sessions waiting for a lock or pin report a *library cache lock* or *library cache pin* wait respectively. The parameters for these waits are shown in Table 4-5.

Table 4-5. Wait Parameters (library cache lock and library cache pin waits)

Parameter	Description
p1	The address in memory of the library cache handle.
p2	The memory address of the lock or pin structure.
p3	The mode of lock or pin required, and the namespace of the object, encoded as 10 * *mode* + *namespace*. In this case, the modes are: 3 shared 5 exclusive The namespaces are: 0 cursor 1 table, procedure, and others 2 package body 3 trigger 4 index 5 cluster 6 object 7 pipe

If there are multiple readers of a single pipe, then library cache pin waits on the library cache object for that pipe will be routine, but brief. Other than that, library cache waits are relatively rare, although much more likely to be prolonged. These waits time out after three seconds and, if they do time out, deadlock detection is performed. If a deadlock is found, the lock or pin request is aborted and an ORA-4020 error is returned. This error is normally caused by ad hoc DDL. It should not be necessary to code your applications to handle this error.

DML Locks

Library cache pins and the associated row cache enqueue locks protect object definitions for the duration of parse and execute calls. However, for transactions that consist of a series of statements, equivalent locks need to be held for the duration of the transaction.

More than that, the lock mode may need to be raised partway through the transaction. For example, a table may first be queried, and then updated. This, of course, is why lock conversions are necessary. If the existing lock were to be released, even momentarily, it would be possible for the referenced object to be dropped or changed, and the transaction would then be unable to either proceed or roll back.

The possibility of rollback, particularly rollback to a savepoint, adds another dimension of complexity to dictionary locking. Namely, if a transaction is rolled back beyond the point at which a lock was upgraded, then the lock must be downgraded correspondingly, as part of the rollback operation, in order to reduce the risk of artificial deadlocks.

The requirements of dictionary locking for transactions and, in particular, the maintenance of a history of lock conversions, is provided by DML locks in conjunction with TM enqueues. Every transaction holding a DML lock also holds a TM enqueue lock. The basic locking functionality is provided by the enqueue, and the DML lock adds the maintenance of the conversion history.

The fixed array of DML lock structures is sized by the DML_LOCKS parameter. Its free list is protected by the *dml lock allocation* latch, and the active slots are visible in V$LOCKED_OBJECT. As with enqueue resources and locks, the number of slots in the DML locks fixed array is unimportant to performance, as long as you don't run out of free slots and get an ORA-55 error. Once again, V$RESOURCE_LIMIT can be used to adjust your setting for DML_LOCKS to ensure that this does not happen. Each slot only takes on the order of 116 bytes, so having a generous number of slots is not a problem.

Disabling DML Locks

DML locks and the associated TM enqueue locks can be disabled, either entirely, or just for certain tables. To disable these locks entirely, the DML_LOCKS parameter must be set to zero. In a parallel server database, it must be set to zero in all instances. To disable such locks against a particular table, the DISABLE TABLE LOCKS clause of the ALTER TABLE statement must be used.

If locks are disabled for a table, then DML statements can still modify the table's blocks, and row-level locks are still held. However, the sub-shared mode table locks normally associated with queries, and the sub-exclusive mode table locks normally associated with DML, are not taken. Instead, transactions against the table are protected from conflicting DDL by simply prohibiting all attempts to take a lock on the entire table, and thus all DDL against the table.

There are two reasons for disabling DML locks and table locks. The first is to avoid the lock acquisition overhead. This is particularly important in parallel server databases where the transactions are short. In such cases, it may take longer to acquire the TM instance lock than to complete the rest of the transaction.

In single-instance Oracle, the lock acquisition overhead is relatively trivial. However, the disabling of table locks should still be considered to efficiently prevent blocking lock problems. A large class of blocking lock problems is caused by attempts to lock an entire table, sometimes for ad hoc DDL such as creating an index, but often for ad hoc DML against a referenced table where the relationship is not supported by a foreign key index.

Foreign keys referring to tiny reference tables are often indexed to prevent such problems. However, the presence of such indexes adds a significant overhead to DML against the main table. It is better to do without these indexes, and prevent blocking locks by disabling table locks. Of course, table locks will need to be enabled temporarily for maintenance tasks such as updating the reference data or rebuilding indexes. However, that is no hardship, as such operations are normally performed during a special maintenance window.

Of course, it is preferable to disable table locks on each table individually, rather than to disable them entirely by setting the DML_LOCKS parameter to zero. If DML_LOCKS is zero, you can create temporary tables but never drop them, and you have to shut down and start up the system twice for maintenance operations such as rebuilding indexes.

Buffer Locks

A form of enqueue locking is used to protect cached database blocks. For each buffer in the database buffer cache, there is a buffer header. The buffer headers constitute a fixed array in the permanent memory part of the shared pool. These buffer headers act as the resource structures for buffer locks. Sessions manipulate buffer headers, and thus buffers, via dynamically allocated structures known as buffer handles. The buffer handles act as the lock structures for buffer locks.

Buffer locks are taken only in shared and exclusive modes.* The buffer headers implement a two-way linked list of the buffer handles for sessions that are using the buffer, and another for the buffer handles of sessions waiting for the buffer. Sessions waiting for a buffer lock report either *buffer busy waits*, or *buffer busy due to global cache* waits, or *write complete waits*. The parameters for *buffer busy waits* are shown in Table 4-6.

Table 4-6. Wait Parameters (buffer busy waits)

Parameter	Description
p1	The file number of the database block.
p2	The block number of the database block in its file.
p3	The reason for the wait. A 0 or 1014 indicates that the buffer is locked exclusively by a session that is busy reading a block from disk into the buffer, and that the read has not yet completed. A reason of 0 is used for consistent gets, whereas 1014 is used for current mode block gets. Any other number indicates that the buffer is locked exclusively for modification by another session.

The timeout for *buffer busy waits* backs off from 1 to 3 seconds. If a buffer lock for a block that is in cache cannot be acquired within a certain number of timeouts, and if the session is holding buffer locks on one or more other buffers, then a buffer lock deadlock is assumed. The number of timeouts to wait before a buffer lock deadlock is assumed is dependent on the operation being attempted, and whether it is part of a discrete transaction. Because discrete transactions do not hold transaction locks, and thus row-level locks, they must acquire all the buffer locks they need before any modifications can be made, and hold them all until the transaction is ready to make its changes and commit. This means that discrete transactions hold more buffer locks than normal transactions, and hold them for much longer.

---

* This is a simplification, but adequate for our purpose here.

If a buffer lock deadlock is suspected, the session that timed out trying to acquire a buffer lock releases the buffer locks that it is holding on other buffers, and immediately enqueues them again, thereby falling to the end of the queue of waiting sessions. It also posts the first process that was waiting for a lock on each of the buffers concerned, and then yields the CPU. Although yielding the CPU does not really constitute a wait, a *buffer deadlock* wait is recorded and the *exchange deadlocks* statistic is incremented. Assumed buffer lock deadlocks signal event 370, which can be caught to investigate such problems.

In parallel server databases, buffers can be locked for global cache operations such as writes in response to ping requests, and consistent reads for direct memory transfers by the block server process. If a request for a buffer lock cannot proceed because the buffer is locked for a global cache operation, then a *buffer busy due to global cache* wait is recorded.

Similarly, when buffer lock requests cannot proceed because the buffers are locked by DBWn as part of a batch of blocks to be written, then *write complete waits* are recorded. The timeout for these waits is 1 second, and the parameters are as shown in Table 4-7.

Table 4-7. Wait Parameters (write complete waits)

Parameter	Description
p1	The file number of the database block.
p2	The block number of the database block in its file.
p3	The reason for the wait. The normal reason code is 1029; however, other values are seen at times.

Sort Locks

Sort locks apply to the disk space being used for disk sort operations. There are two types of sort locks: temporary table locks and sort segment locks. These correspond to temporary segments in PERMANENT tablespaces and TEMPORARY tablespaces respectively. There are fixed arrays in the SGA for each type of sort lock. Both arrays are sized by the SESSIONS parameter, which allows for the maximum possible usage of sort locks.

Sort locks are used merely to track disk sort space usage, and do not suffer from lock conflicts, waits, or deadlocks. However, you should not confuse sort locks with the ST (space transaction) enqueue, which is extremely prone to lock conflicts, waits, and even deadlocks. Contention for the ST enqueue is often associated with disk sorts, because it is needed for the creation, extension, and deallocation of temporary segments.

Reference

This section contains a quick reference to the parameters, events, statistics, waits, and APT scripts mentioned in Chapter 4.

Parameters

Parameter	Description
_DISTRIBUTED_LOCK_TIMEOUT	Timeout for assumed deadlocks on distributed transactions. Defaults to 60 seconds.
_ENQUEUE_HASH	The size of the enqueue hash table.
_ENQUEUE_HASH_CHAIN_LATCHES	The number of latches used for access to the enqueue hash table. Defaults to the CPU count.
_ENQUEUE_LOCKS	The number of enqueue lock structures.
DML_LOCKS	The size of the DML locks fixed array. Where possible, DML locking should be disabled to reduce locking overheads and the risk of blocking locks.
ENQUEUE_RESOURCES	The size of the enqueue resources array.
PARALLEL_TRANSACTION_ RESOURCE_TIMEOUT	Timeout for assumed deadlocks between the branches of a parallel transaction and another transaction in release 8.0.
TEMPORARY_TABLE_LOCKS	This parameter is obsolete in Oracle8. It does still exist in release 8.0, but setting it has no effect.

Events

Event	Description
60	This is the enqueue deadlock detection error. In cases of recurrent, mysterious deadlock problems, you may need to take a systemstate dump on this event to diagnose the interactions causing the deadlocks.
370	This event is signaled for assumed buffer cache deadlocks, and can be used for investigating severe buffer locking contention, using processstate dumps.
4020	This is the library cache deadlock detection error. With a systemstate dump on this event, you will be able to see what happened. Without it, you will never know.
4021	This is the library cache assumed deadlock timeout error. This timeout is needed because the library cache deadlock detection mechanism is not exhaustive, lest it be too expensive. Once again, this error is normally caused by ad hoc DDL.

Statistics

Statistic	Source	Description
enqueue conversions	V$SYSSTAT	Local enqueue conversions.
enqueue deadlocks	V$SYSSTAT	Local enqueue deadlocks detected and broken.
enqueue releases	V$SYSSTAT	Local enqueue releases.
enqueue requests	V$SYSSTAT	Local enqueue requests.
enqueue timeouts	V$SYSSTAT	Aborted local enqueue operations.
enqueue waits	V$SYSSTAT	The number of enqueue operations that waited. Not the number of waits.
exchange deadlocks	V$SYSSTAT	Number of local buffer deadlocks assumed. The statistic name reflects the fact that index block exchanges are one possible cause of such deadlocks.

Waits

Event	Description
buffer busy due to global cache	Waits to acquire a local buffer lock on a buffer that is locked for a global cache operation, such as a ping.
buffer busy waits	Waits for a local buffer lock on a buffer that is locked in an incompatible mode.
buffer deadlock	Assumed deadlocks while waiting for a local buffer lock.
enqueue	These are waits for both local and global enqueues.
library cache load lock	This wait is seen if two sessions attempt to load (not reload) the library cache information for an object simultaneously. Simultaneous reloads cause library cache pin waits instead.
library cache lock	Waits to reference a library cache object that is in flux.
library cache pin	Waits to modify a library cache object that is in flux.
row cache lock	Waits to obtain either a local row cache enqueue or a row cache instance lock.
write complete waits	Waits for a buffer lock on a block that is part of a normal write batch.

APT Scripts

Script	Description
enqueue_locks.sql	Shows enqueue locks held and wanted in the order requested.
enqueue_stats.sql	Shows the breakdown of enqueue gets and waits by type.
fixed_table_hwms.sql	Shows the high-water mark usage for the fixed tables under Oracle7. This can be used to check whether your settings for the corresponding initialization parameters are inadequate or overly generous. Under Oracle8, use V$RESOURCE_LIMIT instead.

5

Instance Locks

Instance locks are used for inter-instance locking and communication between the instances of an Oracle parallel server database. Although instance locks are scarcely used in single-instance Oracle, I encourage all readers to browse this chapter anyway. Single-instance Oracle is really just a special case of parallel server, and there are some aspects of its operation that you will find difficult to grasp unless you understand the general case. If nothing else, reading this chapter will deepen your appreciation for the simplicity of single-instance Oracle.

The Lock Manager

The part of Oracle that manages instance locks is called the lock manager. The lock manager is a layer of functionality that affects the operation of all processes. However, its most obvious manifestations are the presence of a set of lock management processes, and an in-memory database of instance lock information in each instance.

The lock manager is said to be *distributed*. There is no central point of control. Each instance only maintains information about the instance locks in which it has an interest. The lock manager is also said to be *integrated*. This is because, prior to Oracle8, a separate product provided by the operating system vendors was required for lock management. In Oracle8, release 8.0, this functionality was incorporated into the Oracle kernel.

The Instance Lock Database

The lock and resource structures for instance locks reside in a dedicated area within the SGA called the instance lock database. The lock and resource arrays are dimensioned by the LM_LOCKS and LM_RESS parameters. A third parameter, LM_PROCS, dimensions the array of processes and instances that can own the locks. This array needs one slot for each local process and one slot for each remote instance.

The instance lock database also includes an array of process groups. In some cases, instance locks may be owned by a group of processes, rather than a single process. Group lock ownership allows Multi-Threaded Server sessions to migrate between shared server processes, and allows OCI transactions to be detached from one process and resumed by a different process. All lock acquisition requests can specify either process or group ownership. The group membership of processes is inferred and tracked automatically in the instance lock database. Exchanges of group-owned instance locks within the process group do not require any further lock acquisition or conversion. The size of the process groups array is set by the _LM_GROUPS parameter, which defaults to 20.

The instance lock database contains many other structures besides the resources, locks, processes, and process groups. There are hash tables for access to many of these arrays; structures for recording statistics, managing waits and timeouts, checking for deadlocks, and performing recovery; and also a large portion of memory to hold the message buffers used for inter-instance communication. The number of buffers is set by the _LM_SEND_BUFFERS parameter, which defaults to 10,000.

Most parts of the instance lock database are fixed in size from instance startup. However, Oracle has the option of allocating memory from the shared pool for additional dynamically allocated resources and locks if necessary. If this occurs, a message is written to the alert log, and the corresponding parameter should be increased prior to the next database startup, unless the overrun was due to the recovery of another instance. The GV$RESOURCE_LIMIT view contains statistics about the number of dynamic resources and locks allocated, as does GV$DLM_MISC. Note that the dynamically allocated memory is never released back into the shared pool.

Lock Mastering

The instance lock database is a distributed database. No single node tracks all the locks on all the resources. For each resource there is a master node. The master node for a resource maintains complete information about all the locks on that resource. Other nodes need only maintain information about locally held locks on that resource. For dynamically allocated resources, the master node is normally the first node to take a lock on the resource. There is also a directory node for each resource, which maintains a pointer to the master node. The directory node is determined using a hash function based on the resource identification. For persistent resources, the master node is always the directory node.

Whenever the set of active instances changes due to instance startup or shutdown, or due to the failure of an instance or node, then the distribution of resources to nodes must be changed. In general, both the directory node and the master node for each resource might change, and the required information must be reconstructed at each node. If an instance has failed, then the roll forward phase of instance recovery (called cache recovery) must also be completed before all instance lock information can be validated.

The instance lock database is frozen during both resource redistribution and cache recovery, if applicable. During this time, local activity may continue, but only under the instance locks that were already held. However, if an instance has been lost, local activity is limited to read-only access to data already in memory, and for which an instance lock was already held. This is an extremely severe constraint. You should attempt to limit the time required for resource redistribution and instance recovery roll forward by using modest numbers of resources and locks, and by configuring checkpoint activity to ensure bounded recovery times.

Lock Handle Acquisition

Many instance locks are acquired in two steps. The first step is to obtain a lock handle, which is an identifier of the lock to be used in subsequent conversion or release operations. Some instance locks are held for the life of the instance and are never converted or released. These locks are acquired in a single step, and no lock handle is returned.

Although the lock manager has been integrated into the Oracle kernel, processes needing a lock handle do not access the instance lock database to allocate a lock handle directly. Instead, they still construct and send a message to the LMDn background process, and wait for LMDn to return a lock handle. The message identifies the resource, and sets certain options that govern both the acquisition of the lock and its subsequent management.

If the resource does not exist in the local instance lock database, then a slot is allocated from the instance lock resource table. The resource may be marked as persistent, if it is to be retained once all locks have been released. The directory node is computed from the resource identification, and the master node is marked as unknown (unless the resource is persistent). Once the resource exists in the local instance lock database, a slot in the instance lock table is allocated to the lock. Its process or group ownership is established, and deadlock detection parameters are set. The LMDn background process then constructs and sends a reply message to the client process. This message is called an acquisition asynchronous trap, or acquisition AST. The acquisition AST message includes a lock handle.

Processes waiting for LMDn to return a lock handle wait on a *DFS lock handle* wait. DFS stands for Distributed File System, which is an old name for Oracle's instance lock management functionality. Lock handle waits should be brief, because they are resolved entirely locally. If these waits take longer than 1 centisecond on average, then the LMDn process is overworked.

Instance Lock Acquisition

Once a lock handle has been obtained, the process needing an instance lock constructs and sends a second message to LMDn to convert the lock. This message identifies the lock handle, specifies the new lock mode required, and sets further options. If the master node for the resource is already known, this message may be sent directly to the LMDn process at the master node depending on the setting of the _LM_DIRECT_SENDS parameter which defaults to ALL in release 8.1, but just to LKMGR in release 8.0.

If the master node for the resource is still unknown, the local LMDn sends a message to the directory node to find out which node is the master node for this resource. If a master node has not already been assigned, the directory node assigns a master node. Depending on the resource type, the lock mastering is either assigned to all active nodes cyclically, or to the originating instance if the resource is unlikely to be used from other instances. Once the master node is known, the acquisition or conversion request can be forwarded to the master node.

If the lock information held at the master node indicates that the lock can be granted immediately, then the lock is linked into the granted queue at both the master node and locally, and a conversion AST message is returned to the client process via the LMDn process of the client instance. Otherwise, the lock is linked to the convert queue for the resource, and the client process continues to wait.

When a lock request is blocked, the LMDn process at the master node may ask the blocking lock holders to downgrade the modes of their locks on the resource, in order to allow the new conversion request to be granted. This is done by sending a blocking asynchronous trap, or BAST, to the blocking processes and instances. Whether a lock holder is able to receive BAST messages, and the level to which it may be willing to downgrade its lock, are set during lock acquisition or conversion. When a blocking process has complied with a BAST, it sends a completion AST in reply.

The GV$DLM_LOCKS view shows the details for all blocked and blocking locks in the instance lock database, including all the options set when acquiring and converting the locks. GV$DLM_ALL_LOCKS shows the same details, but for all instance locks, including those held in null mode.

LCKn Processes

Many instance locks are not obtained directly by the process requiring the lock. Instead, the LCKn processes obtain them on behalf of the entire instance. The LCKn processes operate asynchronously. That is, when they send requests to the LMDn process, they do not wait for an acquisition or conversion AST to be returned. Instead, they are available to handle further lock requests from other processes. This is why a distinction is made in the GV$SYSSTAT statistics between asynchronous and synchronous global lock gets and conversions.

By default, only one LCKn process is started. This is normally sufficient, because it operates asynchronously. However, if LCK0 is very active, and if the operating system does not support priority fixing, then LCK0 may have to queue for the CPU, thereby degrading overall system performance. If so, multiple LCKn processes can be started using the _GC_LCK_ PROCS parameter.

Lock Value Blocks

When a process acquires or converts an instance lock, it can read or write the 16-byte lock value block which is maintained in the resource structure at the master node. For example, the lock value block of the SM (SMON) instance lock resource represents the last time an SMON process ran in any instance. The lock value block facility is also used to communicate System Change Numbers (SCNs) between instances, and to establish parallel execution communication paths. However, the lock value block is not used for most resource types.

Incidentally, the resource structure for local enqueues also includes a lock value block, but it is scarcely ever used.

Global Locks

Many of the resources protected by local locks in single-instance Oracle require global exposure in a parallel server database. Whenever one of these local locks is needed, a corresponding instance lock must be held as well, to protect the resource across all instances. The instance locks used to protect local locks globally are called *global locks*. However, the term is sometimes used informally as a synonym for all instance locks generally.

Row Cache Instance Locks

Row cache instance locks correspond directly to local row cache enqueue locks. They do not supersede the local locks, but give them global exposure.

When a process needs a row cache instance lock, it posts the LCK0 background process to obtain the lock on behalf of the instance, and waits on a *row cache lock* wait. This same wait is also recorded when waiting for the corresponding local lock. LCK0 obtains the instance lock asynchronously. When LCK0 receives the acquisition or conversion AST from LMDn, it posts the waiting process.

When the local process releases its row cache enqueue lock, the dictionary row remains cached, and so the instance lock is not released but downgraded to null mode in the background by the LCK0 process. However, the row cache instance lock is released if the dictionary cache entry is flushed from the shared pool.

Although dictionary cache entries and row cache enqueue locks are dynamically allocated in the shared pool, the lock state information for the corresponding instance locks is not. That information is maintained in a fixed array which is dimensioned by the _ROW_CACHE_INSTANCE_ LOCKS parameter. The size of this array limits the number of null mode instance locks cached by each instance, and thus constrains the resource usage in the instance lock database for row cache instance locks. Consider increasing the size of this array to cache a working set of instance locks if the GV$ROWCACHE view shows ongoing DLM_RELEASES without many DLM_CONFLICTS.

Global Enqueues

Most of the resources protected by enqueue locks in single-instance Oracle have global exposure in a parallel server database. These are the global enqueues.

Global enqueue locks are taken by the foreground and background processes taking the local locks. They are not taken by the LCKn processes on behalf of the instance. The instance lock resources for global enqueues are dynamically assigned, and like the local enqueue resources, they are not persistent. Most global enqueue resource types are mastered locally, because locks on these resources are seldom needed by other instances.

The single most effective way to optimize global enqueue locking is to disable table locking. Indeed, this is strongly recommended for Oracle parallel server. The preferred way of doing this is to use the ALTER TABLE DISABLE TABLE LOCK command on all application tables, rather than setting the DML_LOCKS parameter to 0, as discussed in the previous chapter.

Cross-Instance Calls

One global enqueue type is worthy of particular mention because of its role in inter-instance communication. Some operations, such as changing the backup state of tablespaces, log file operations, global checkpoints, and others, need global coordination because all the instances must cooperate in performing the operation.

This communication between instances is effected using CI (cross-instance call) enqueues. For each type of operation, the background processes of each instance hold instance locks on a set of resources. By manipulating the modes of these locks, it is possible to trigger global actions and wait for them to be completed.

For example, prior to performing a direct read operation on a database segment, the reader process or parallel query coordinator uses a cross-instance call to the DBWn processes requesting a checkpoint of all dirty cached blocks belonging to that segment. The lock value block is used to communicate the database object number for the segment. Similarly, before truncating a segment, reuse block range cross-instance calls are used to ensure that dirty cached blocks within the affected range have been flushed to disk, and that clean cached blocks within the affected range have been invalidated.

Despite their name, many cross-instance calls are used, and the corresponding CI enqueues are taken in single-instance Oracle as well as in a parallel server.

Library Cache Instance Locks

Some library cache locks and pins also have global exposure in a parallel server database. Remember that library cache locks are held during parse calls, and that pins are held during execute calls, to prevent conflicting DDL. In parallel server databases it is necessary to prevent such conflicting DDL in all instances. To achieve this, it is sufficient to globally expose the library cache locks and pins on database objects only. The local locks and pins on dependent objects such as cursors do not need global exposure, because they are indirectly protected if all the database objects on which they depend are protected.

Remember further that local library cache locks are retained in null mode to invalidate cached library cache objects should the definition of an object on which they depend be changed. The same functionality is provided between instances, on database objects only, by the LCK0 processes holding an IV (invalidation) instance lock in shared mode on all database objects cached in the library cache. Any process that needs to invalidate an object definition globally merely takes an exclusive mode lock on the same resource, thereby causing the LCK0 processes to drop their shared lock and invalidate the object.

The use of global library cache locks, pins, and invalidation locks can be disabled using hidden parameters. This is not recommended unless DML locks have also been completely disabled.

PCM Instance Locks

Parallel cache management (PCM) instance locks do *not* protect cache buffers—at least not directly. They protect data structures known as *lock elements*. Each lock element protects a set of data blocks, not cache buffers. However, any cache buffers containing those data blocks are linked to their lock element.

Lock elements are also called global cache locks, but that term is unhelpful because they are neither locks nor resources. They are an intersection entity between PCM instance locks and cache buffers.

Fixed Lock Elements

Lock elements are either releasable or fixed. Releasable lock elements may be used for either hashed or fine-grained locking, but fixed lock elements are used only for hashed locking. In hashed locking, data blocks are mapped to lock elements using a hash algorithm, and a single lock element may protect any number of cached blocks at once. In fine-grained locking, lock elements are dynamically allocated to protect a single cached block at a time.

The mapping of data blocks to hashed lock elements, and whether they are fixed or releasable lock elements, is established by the GC_FILES_TO_ LOCKS and GC_ROLLBACK_LOCKS parameters. The number of fixed lock elements is derived from these strings. The number of releasable lock elements used for hashed locking in these strings must be less than the number of releasable lock elements specified with the GC_RELEASABLE_ LOCKS parameter, which defaults to the number of buffers in the cache. The remaining releasable lock elements are available for fine-grained locking.

Fixed and releasable hashed locking exhibit identical performance, except in one very important respect. During instance startup, the LCKn processes must acquire null mode instance locks on all fixed lock elements. This can take many minutes. Releasable hashed locking diffuses this cost over an initial ramp-up phase of instance activity. Thereafter, the performance of these two forms of hashed locking are identical. Note that the lock handles on releasable hashed lock elements are never actually released, despite the lock elements being releasable. In view of this, you should only use releasable lock elements for hashed locking, and should not use fixed lock elements at all.

Hashed Locking

When a block is brought into the cache, the lock element under which it will be protected must be determined, and the buffer must be linked to that lock element. How this is done depends on whether the block uses fine-grained or hashed locking, and in the case of hashed locking, it also depends on the class of the block. Rollback segment blocks and data blocks are treated separately.

For data blocks subject to hashed locking, there is an index array that maps file numbers to lock element buckets, and a bucket header array that identifies the series of lock elements in each bucket. These arrays are visible as X$KCLFI and X$KCLFH. For rollback segment blocks, the corresponding arrays are X$KCLUI and X$KCLUH. These arrays are constructed from the GC_FILES_TO_LOCKS and GC_ROLLBACK_LOCKS parameters during instance startup.

When a rollback segment block or data block is brought into cache, these arrays are used to look up the correct lock element bucket. No latching is necessary, because the arrays are static. The lock element chosen to protect a particular block from within its bucket is the block number minus two, divided by the blocking factor for the bucket, divided by the number of lock elements in the bucket, rounded down. This hash function subtracts two from the block number, rather than one, to allow for the file header block and to thereby ensure that if the blocking factor is chosen as an integer divisor of the extent size expressed in blocks, then lock element coverage will align to extent boundaries. Further, it is good practice to make the number of lock elements in each bucket a prime number to ensure an even distribution of blocks to lock elements, regardless of the data distribution within database segments.

A heavier concentration of lock elements should be allocated to data files that may be subject to contention for hashed PCM instance locks. The risk of such contention is greatest on data files whose blocks are subject to change and whose blocks are accessed from multiple instances.

Fine-Grained Locking

Data files and rollback segments that are not assigned any hashed lock elements in GC_FILES_TO_LOCKS and GC_ROLLBACK_LOCKS, or that are explicitly given no lock elements, use fine-grained locking unless an alternative default bucket (bucket 0) has also been defined. In fine-grained locking each data block is protected by a dedicated lock element from the set of unassigned releasable lock elements. Because just one data block is protected by each lock element at any one time, fine-grained locking is also called DBA (data block address) locking. Fine-grained locking is also used for all block classes other than data blocks and rollback segment blocks. These minor block classes include segment header blocks, free list blocks, and extent map blocks.

If fine-grained locking is being used for certain data files, and if important minor class blocks such as segment header blocks are often aged out of the buffer cache, then the lock elements for those blocks may be reused before their blocks are read in again. This results in unnecessary instance lock acquisition and resource allocation overhead. In this case, to improve the retention of instance locks, you should consider reserving a number of lock elements in a separate bucket for the minor class blocks by setting the _GC_CLASS_LOCKS parameter.

The Lock Element Free List

When a block subject to fine-grained locking is brought into the cache, a hash table is consulted to determine whether a lock element for the block has been preserved. This is done under the protection of the *KCL name table latch*. If necessary, a lock element is allocated from the LRU (least recently used) end of the lock element LRU chain under the protection of the *KCL freelist latch*. Note that despite the name of this latch, the data structure that it protects is an LRU chain of both free and in use (named) lock elements. The term, lock element free list, is just another name for the set of free lock elements at the end of the lock element LRU chain.

In most instances, it is desirable to have lock elements available on the free list at all times. The X$KCLFX fixed table contains some free list statistics. In particular, the LWM column contains the low-water mark of the free list length. This can be seen with the APT script *lock_element_lwm.sql*. Lock elements are returned to the MRU (most recently used) end of the LRU chain when their protected buffer is reused. Lock elements may be reclaimed from the free list if the protected block is brought back into cache before the lock element has been reused.

In very large memory (VLM) environments, it may be desirable to have fewer lock elements available than the number of cache buffers under fine-grained locking. It is not that there is not ample memory available for the lock elements and instance locks, but that having a large number of instance locks would greatly extend the period of reduced availability during instance lock redistribution when necessary. In such environments, named lock elements are reused in LRU order as required. If a process has to wait while a lock element is prepared for reuse, it waits on a *global cache freelist wait*. The only parameter to this wait is the lock element number.

PCM Lock Acquisition

When a block is brought into cache, a buffer from the buffer cache LRU chain is selected for reuse, and the session allocates a buffer handle to work with the buffer. First it must unlink the buffer header from the lock element under which the previous block cached in that buffer was protected, if any. Then it must link the buffer header to the lock element for the new block. These operations are performed under the protection of the *KCL lock element parent latch* for that lock element.

If multiple LCKn processes have been configured, then the lock element array is partitioned between these processes, and a separate set of lock element parent latches is used for each partition. The number of latches in each set is determined by the _GC_LATCHES parameter, which defaults amply to two times the CPU count.

Of course, more needs to be done than merely linking the buffer for a new block to its lock element. In particular, a PCM instance lock of the correct mode needs to be acquired on the lock element. The LCKn background processes perform this task. For fine-grained locks, they must also release the instance lock and resource previously held for that lock element.

When a foreground process needs to acquire or convert a PCM instance lock on a particular lock element, it allocates a structure called a lock context object. The lock context object is linked to the lock element, and fully describes the operation to be performed. The foreground process then posts the LCKn process and waits for the LCKn process to complete the locking operation and clean up the lock context object.

While the foreground process is waiting for LCKn to obtain a lock, it sleeps on one of the *global cache lock* waits. The timeout for these waits is 1 second. The parameters are as shown in Table 5-1.

Table 5-1. Wait Parameters (global cache lock waits)

Parameter	Description
p1	The file number of the database block.
p2	The block number of the database block in its file.
p3	The lock element number, or the block class for minor class block lock acquisitions.

While a process is waiting on a global cache lock wait because a blocking lock is held by a remote instance, the details can be seen in GV$DLM_LOCKS. The resource name is constructed from the lock type and the two lock identifiers. The lock type for PCM instance locks is BL (block lock). The first identifier is the lock element number for hashed locking, and the data block address for fine-grained locking. The second identifier is the block class, as shown in Table 5-2.

Table 5-2. Block Classes

Block Class	Class Description
1	Data blocks
2	Sort blocks

Table 5-2. Block Classes (continued)

Block Class	Class Description
3	Deferred rollback segment blocks
4	Segment header blocks
5	Deferred rollback segment header blocks
6	Free list blocks
7	Extent map blocks
8	Space management bitmap blocks
9	Space management index blocks
10	Unused
$11 + 2r$	Segment header block for rollback segment r
$12 + 2r$	Data blocks for rollback segment r

Block Pings

If a remote instance needs a PCM instance lock in an incompatible mode with the lock held locally, then the LCKn process holding that lock will receive a BAST from the local LMDn process. If none of the blocks protected by that lock element are currently in the cache, or if they are in cache but in a compatible state, then the LCKn process can downgrade its lock mode immediately. However, if any blocks protected by the lock element are in cache in an incompatible state, then the lock cannot be downgraded until after the block states have been changed. Changing the state of a cached block in response to a BAST is called a *ping*.

Cached blocks can be in three possible states.* First, they can be current or stale. Stale copies of blocks are kept in the cache to satisfy long-running queries. Queries need to perform consistent reads. That is, blocks that have been modified since the query started need to be rolled back, so that the information returned by the query will reflect a consistent snap-shot of the database at the time that the query or transaction began. Retaining stale copies of blocks in cache for consistent reads reduces the need to roll back changes for queries. Because of this, stale copies of blocks that are still in the cache are said to be in consistent read (CR) state. Note that CR is also the abbreviation for the concurrent read lock mode, which can be cause for confusion at times.

Cached blocks that are not stale are current. Current blocks can be in two states, namely clean or dirty. A current block is dirty if it has been

---

* Note that I am speaking here of block states. The states of the buffers containing those blocks are related, but different.

changed and still has to be written to disk. A current block is clean if it does not contain changes that still have to be written to disk.

Pings only affect current blocks. If a remote instance requires a shared lock on a lock element, then any dirty blocks protected by that lock element locally need to be written to disk and thus cleaned. When these blocks have been cleaned, the local lock on that lock element can be downgraded to shared mode. However, if the remote instance needs to change a block, then it will request an exclusive lock on its lock element. Any dirty blocks protected by that lock element locally need to be written to disk, and clean blocks must be marked as stale; that is, they must be converted to consistent read state. The local lock on the lock element can then be downgraded to null mode.

Pings that affect dirty blocks and cause them to be written to disk are called *hard pings*. Pings that only affect the state of blocks, by causing them to be marked as stale, are called *soft pings*. Hard pings are a form of forced write. Forced writes also occur in response to checkpoint object, reuse block range, and write buffer cross-instance calls. Soft pings are a form of cache invalidation, which is forcing a block to become stale. This term reflects the fact that the cache buffer no longer contains a valid current copy of the block. Cache invalidations also occur in response to reuse block range cross-instance calls. Forced reads, as shown in GV$BH, are cases when an instance had to read a block back into cache after it was invalidated.

Under hashed locking, it is possible for multiple cached blocks to be affected by a single ping. Similarly, it is possible for blocks other than the block required by the remote instance to be affected by a ping. Pings of blocks other than the block required by the remote instance are called *false pings*. *True pings* are those in which the only block affected is the block required by the remote instance. Fine-grained locking is not subject to false pings, because only one block is protected under each lock element.

Pings are a major performance issue for parallel server databases. The fixed table GV$FILE_PING contains detailed statistics about pings that have occurred for each data file, as well as other forced writes and invalidations. This information is invaluable in pinpointing trouble spots while tuning a parallel server database to reduce pings.

Consistent Read Requests

Oracle uses several optimizations to reduce the number of pings and their impact. Queries only need consistent read copies of the data blocks, not necessarily the current block image. If a stale copy of the block that is more recent than the consistent read SCN for the query is available in the local cache, then that copy will be used. If the lock element is not locked in exclusive mode by another instance, then a shared mode lock is taken and the block is read from disk and rolled back as required. However, if an exclusive lock is held by another instance, Oracle must obtain a suitable read consistent copy of the block from that instance. How this is done depends on the Oracle release.

In release 8.0, Oracle first attempts to ping the block. However, if the block is very hot in the remote instance, the ping request times out after 6 seconds (or the value of the _CR_DEADTIME parameter). In this case, Oracle uses a write buffer cross-instance call to trigger the remote DBWn to write the current buffer to disk. The block can then be read from disk and rolled back as required. However, the rollback operation commonly requires several more calls for rollback segment blocks from the remote instance.

In release 8.1, Oracle uses an alternative cross-instance call to trigger the remote block server process to construct the required consistent read copy of the block and transfer it directly to the client instance. If, however, the remote instance no longer has a current copy of the block in its cache, then the client instance is given permission to read the current image of the block from disk and perform the required rollback itself. This is reflected in the *global cache cr blocks received* and *global cache cr blocks read from disk* statistics.

Oracle plans to extend the block service feature to include transfers of current mode blocks in a later release.

Deferred Ping Responses

Another optimization that Oracle uses to reduce the impact of pings is to defer its response to hard pings by 10 centiseconds, or by the setting of the GC_DEFER_TIME parameter. This is often long enough to allow the active transaction to complete its current series of changes to the block, and mark them as complete within the block header, so that the remote instance will not have to check that transaction's status immediately after reading the block. Checking the status of a remote transaction is an expensive operation, because it requires a ping of the transaction's rollback segment header block, which is invariably a very hot block.

Tuning GC_DEFER_TIME is a matter of balancing the number of pings against the response time for pings, and it can be tuned conveniently because it is a dynamic parameter with ALTER SYSTEM scope. However, local operations on a lock element may be delayed unduly if pings take too long to resolve. In this case *global cache lock busy* waits will be observed. The timeout for this wait is one second, and the wait parameters are the same as for the other global cache lock waits.

Another optimization that Oracle uses to reduce the impact of pings is to automatically queue a conversion request to restore its lock mode after a ping. This can be disabled in release 8.0 using the _UPCONVERT_FROM_ AST parameter. Similarly, Oracle sometimes takes an exclusive lock earlier than necessary to reduce the number of lock conversions. This can be disabled using the _SAVE_ESCALATES parameter. These parameter settings should not normally be changed.

Workload Partitioning

Of course, the best way to reduce pings is to partition the workload so the instances use mutually exclusive sets of data. With a little imagination, and a lot of hard work, it is possible to partition most workloads satisfactorily. One approach, for example, is to use a three-tier architecture with a TP monitor and Oracle's XA libraries to direct global transaction branches to distinct instances based on the data set required.

Another approach worthy of extended consideration is to embrace distributed database technology, in preference to parallel server technology. The overheads of instance locking add significantly to application response times, even under ideal workload partitioning. Those overheads can be eliminated and replaced with more modest network latencies that affect distributed transactions only, as long as you can partition the data as well as the workload into distinct distributed databases.

A parallel server architecture should only be adopted if scalability requirements demand it, and if such complete partitioning of both data and workload into a set of distributed databases is not feasible. The performance of a parallel server database will always be mediocre by comparison with an equivalent distributed or single-instance database. Parallel server is only superior in its scalability under vast workloads.

You must realize, however, that parallel server scalability is not automatic. Careful workload partitioning is essential. Workload partitioning is the key not only to reducing pings, but also to reducing the instance lock acquisition overheads of a parallel server database—in particular, inter-instance message passing.

Blocking Factor

There is one way of improving parallel server scalability that is not immediately obvious, but can result in significant savings both in pings and in
lock acquisition messages.

In hashed locking, although each lock element covers multiple blocks, the
default blocking factor is only one block. For multiblock reads, this means
that a distinct PCM instance lock must be held for each consecutive block.
However, if a blocking factor equal to the multiblock read count is
adopted, then no more than one PCM instance lock will be acquired for
each multiblock read. For globally visible data, this reduces PCM instance
lock acquisition and thus inter-instance messages. This reduction in lock
acquisition also reduces pings for data that is modified. This is because all
the blocks covered by the lock that are cached in an incompatible state in
a remote instance will be released in a single ping operation.

Clearly, a large blocking factor is desirable for data files that contain tables
that are subject to multiblock reads, particularly if they are globally visible
and subject to modification. But if a very large blocking factor is used,
then a large number of buffers will be linked to individual lock elements
at times, introducing a risk of contention for the lock element parent
latches covering those lock elements. Also, if there are hot spots within
the table, a large blocking factor increases the risk of false pings. Nevertheless, a blocking factor of several times the multiblock read count is
normally appropriate for such data files. A generous blocking factor is also
appropriate for rollback segments.

Indexes are much more problematic than tables and rollback segments—
particularly globally visible indexes that are subject to modification. First, it
is imperative that reverse key indexes be used to index monotonically
increasing primary keys, lest considerable contention arise for the PCM
instance lock covering the right-hand leaf block of the index. Oracle
knows few forms of contention so debilitating as this slow motion game
of ping-pong.

For the general case of globally visible and updated indexes, fine-grained
locking is often suggested to combat the risk of false pings. Indeed, in my
opinion, this is the only case in which fine-grained locking should be
considered, and even then you should normally reject it in favor of heavy
hashed locking.

I will concede that heavy hashed locking requires many more lock elements
and instance lock resources and locks. But memory is cheap. Somewhat
more telling is the complaint that heavy hashed locking, because of its

retention of large numbers of instance locks, extends the period of reduced availability during instance lock redistribution when necessary. On the other hand, the database is frozen by default for the transaction recovery phase of instance recovery if any data files use fine-grained locking. This default can be changed with _FREEZE_DB_FOR_FAST_ INSTANCE_RECOVERY if relatively few fine-grained locks are in use. But hashed locking is nevertheless to be preferred if lengthy transaction recovery may be required. However, the decisive argument in favor of heavy hashed locking is that the reduction in locking overhead from the retention of instance locks easily outweighs the performance impact of false pings in almost all cases.

Indexes that are subject to fast full scans also stand to benefit from an increased blocking factor. However, indexes are also more sensitive to false pings than tables, and so a more modest blocking factor is recommended.

In summary, my recommendation is that you use releasable hashed locking for all data files, with a heavier concentration of lock elements on globally visible and updated data.

Other Instance Locks

There are a number of other instance locks used for controlling certain operations in parallel server databases that have no counterpart in single-instance Oracle. For example, the SM (SMON) instance lock is used to ensure that the SMON processes of multiple instances cannot be simultaneously active. This is not necessary in single-instance Oracle. Similarly, the DR (distributed recovery) instance lock is used to ensure that only one RECO process can be active at any one time.

The DF (data file) instance locks are another group of locks that are not needed in single-instance Oracle. There is one DF resource for each data file, and each DBWn process holds a shared mode instance lock on each resource. If a data file is taken offline in one instance, then the remote DBWn processes are notified to no longer attempt to write to that data file by converting the mode of the instance lock on that resource.

Reference

This section contains a quick reference to the parameters, events, statistics, waits, and APT scripts mentioned in Chapter 5.

Parameters

Parameter	Description
_FREEZE_DB_FOR_ FAST_INSTANCE_ RECOVERY	Whether to freeze database activity during the transaction recovery phase of instance recovery. Defaults to TRUE if any data files use fine-grained locking.
_GC_CLASS_LOCKS	The number of releasable lock elements to reserve for fine-grained locking of the minor class blocks.
_GC_LATCHES	The number of lock element latches per partition of the lock elements fixed array. Defaults to two times the number of CPUs, which is ample.
_GC_LCK_PROCS	The number of LCKn processes. Defaults to 1, which is normally sufficient.
_IGNORE_FAILED_ ESCALATES	Attempts to convert a PCM lock straight after a ping appears to fail because Oracle does not know which instance last modified the protected blocks. However, this merely means that the lock value block is invalid and cannot be used for SCN generation. The lock is usable in every other respect, and so the default setting of TRUE should be accepted. This parameter is not available in release 8.1.
_KGL_MULTI_ INSTANCE_ INVALIDATION	This can be set to FALSE to disable global library cache invalidation locks.
_KGL_MULTI_ INSTANCE_LOCK	This can be set to FALSE to disable global library cache locks.
_KGL_MULTI_ INSTANCE_PIN	This can be set to FALSE to disable global library cache pins.
_LM_DIRECT_SENDS	The processes that can send inter-instance messages directly. The 8.0 default of LKMGR means that all messages are sent via LMDn. The 8.1 default value is ALL.
_LM_DLMD_PROCS	The number of LMDn processes.
_LM_DOMAINS	The number of domain structures in the instance lock database. Domains are used for lock redistribution and recovery. Defaults to 2.
_LM_GROUPS	The number of process group structures in the instance lock database. Defaults to 20.
_LM_SEND_ BUFFERS	The number of message buffers in the instance lock database. Defaults to 10000.
_LM_XIDS	The number of transaction structures in the instance lock database. Defaults to 1.1 times the LM_PROCS value.
_ROW_CACHE_ BUFFER_SIZE	The size of the circular buffer in the PGA of the LCK0 process used for row cache instance locking messages.
_ROW_CACHE_ INSTANCE_LOCKS	The size of the row cache instance locks fixed array.

Parameter	Description
_SAVE_ESCALATES	The default setting of TRUE enables early acquisition of more restrictive PCM instance locks than necessary.
_UPCONVERT_FROM_AST	The default setting of TRUE enables the automatic reclamation of PCM instance lock modes lost due to pings. This parameter is not available in release 8.1.
GC_DEFER_TIME	How long to defer response to ping requests. Defaults to 10 centiseconds.
GC_FILES_TO_LOCKS	A string establishing the mapping of files to lock element buckets for hashed locking.
GC_RELEASABLE_LOCKS	The number of releasable lock elements.
GC_ROLLBACK_LOCKS	A string establishing the mapping of rollback segments to lock element buckets for hashed locking.
LM_LOCKS	The number of lock structures in the instance lock database. Defaults to 12000.
LM_PROCS	The number of process structures in the instance lock database. The default is operating system specific.
LM_RESS	The number of resource structures in the instance lock database. Defaults to 6000.
PARALLEL_SERVER	Virtually no memory is allocated to all the instance lock structures unless this parameter is set to TRUE.

Events

Event	Description
10706	This is the trace event for instance lock operations. Level 1 lists the calls; level 5 includes the replies; and level 10 adds time stamps. Expect large trace files.
29700	This event enables the collection of statistics in GV$DLM_CONVERT_LOCAL and GV$DLM_CONVERT_REMOTE.

Statistics

Statistic	Source	Description
cross instance CR read	GV$SYSSTAT	A block required for a query was held under an exclusive lock by another instance. After a ping request timed out, this instance made a cross-instance call for the block. This statistic no longer exists in release 8.1 due to the introduction of cache fusion.
DBWR flush object cross instance calls	GV$SYSSTAT	Number of checkpoint object and invalidate object cross-instance calls.

Statistic	Source	Description
DBWR forced writes	GV$SYSSTAT	Total number of blocks written for forced writes. This statistic was named *DBWR cross instance writes* prior to release 8.1.
global cache convert time	GV$SYSSTAT	PCM instance lock conversion time.
global cache converts	GV$SYSSTAT	PCM instance lock conversions.
global cache cr block receive time	GV$SYSSTAT	The total time for consistent read block requests to be satisfied.
global cache cr blocks read from disk	GV$SYSSTAT	Blocks read from disk for consistent reads because the block had already aged out of the cache of the remote instance holding an exclusive PCM instance lock covering that block.
global cache cr blocks received	GV$SYSSTAT	Consistent read blocks received from remote instances via direct transfer.
global cache defers	GV$SYSSTAT	The number of times a ping request was deferred.
global cache freelist waits	GV$SYSSTAT	Waits to free a lock element for reuse.
global cache get time	GV$SYSSTAT	PCM instance lock acquisition time.
global cache gets	GV$SYSSTAT	PCM instance lock acquisitions.
global cache queued converts	GV$SYSSTAT	PCM instance lock conversions that had to be queued, because another instance was holding the lock in an incompatible mode.
global lock async converts	GV$SYSSTAT	Asynchronous instance lock conversions.
global lock async gets	GV$SYSSTAT	Asynchronous instance lock acquisitions.
global lock convert time	GV$SYSSTAT	Total instance lock conversion time.
global lock get time	GV$SYSSTAT	Total instance lock acquisition time.
global lock releases	GV$SYSSTAT	Instance lock releases.
global lock sync converts	GV$SYSSTAT	Synchronous instance lock conversions.
global lock sync gets	GV$SYSSTAT	Synchronous instance lock acquisitions.
instance recovery database freeze count	GV$SYSSTAT	Global freezes for the transaction recovery phase of instance recovery.

Statistic	Source	Description
remote instance undo block writes	GV$SYSSTAT	Forced writes of rollback segment data blocks.
remote instance undo header writes	GV$SYSSTAT	Forced writes of rollback segment header blocks.
remote instance undo requests	GV$SYSSTAT	Rollback segment block write requests to remote instances needed while rolling back data blocks for consistent reads.
dlm messages sent directly	GV$DLM_MISC	The number of lock management messages sent directly to the target instance by the process needing the lock.
dlm messages flow controlled	GV$DLM_MISC	The number of lock management messages sent indirectly via the local LDMn processes.
dlm messages received	GV$DLM_MISC	The number of lock management messages received by the local LDMn processes.

Waits

Event	Description
DFS lock handle	Waits to obtain a lock handle for an instance lock other than a PCM instance lock.
global cache freelist wait	Waits to free a lock element for reuse.
global cache lock busy	This wait occurs when a PCM instance lock operation cannot proceed because the previous operation on that lock element has not yet completed.
global cache lock open s *global cache lock open x* *global cache lock null to s* *global cache lock null to x* *global cache lock s to x*	Acquiring a PCM instance lock or converting its mode upwards.
global cache lock open ss	Acquiring a PCM instance lock on a minor class block in release 8.0.

APT Scripts

Script	Description
lock_element_ lwm.sql	Shows the low-water mark of the lock element free list

6

Memory

Many tuning issues involve making decisions about memory allocation. Those decisions are complicated by the fact that Oracle manages much of its memory dynamically. To tune Oracle effectively, you need to understand both what it uses memory for and how it manages that memory.

The SGA

The System Global Area (SGA), together with the essential background processes, is definitive of an Oracle instance. It is a global area in the sense that it contains global variables and data structures, and it is a system area in the sense that it contains data structures that must be accessible to the entire Oracle instance, rather than just a particular process.

The SGA Areas

The SGA contains four or five main areas:

- The fixed area
- The variable area
- The database block buffers
- The log buffer
- The instance lock database (for parallel server instances)

In terms of memory size, the fixed area and the log buffer should be trivial.

The fixed area

The fixed area of the SGA contains several thousand atomic variables, small data structures such as latches and pointers into other areas of the SGA. These variables are all listed in the fixed table X$KSMFSV along with their data types, sizes, and memory addresses, as shown in Example 6-1. The names of these SGA variables are cryptic, and seldom of use to know. However, senior Oracle staff can obtain advanced diagnostic information by joining X$KSMFSV with X$KSMMEM to monitor the values of these variables or to probe the data structures that they point to. X$KSMMEM has one row for every memory address in the SGA, and one non-key column which exposes the contents of the memory locations.

Example 6-1. The Redo Allocation Latch as Seen from X$KSMFSV

```
SQL> select ksmfsnam, ksmfstyp, ksmfssiz, ksmfsadr
  2> from x$ksmfsv where ksmfsnam = 'kcrfal_';

KSMFSNAM            KSMFSTYP            KSMFSSIZ   KSMFSADR
------------------  ------------------  ---------- --------
kcrfal_             ksllt                    120 C3F4D13C
```

The size of each component of the fixed area of the SGA is fixed. That is, they are not dependent on the setting of any initialization parameters, or anything else. Thus the offset into the fixed SGA for each variable is fixed, as is the total size of the fixed area itself.

The variable area

The variable area of the SGA is made up of the large pool and the shared pool. All memory in the large pool is dynamically allocated, whereas the shared pool contains both dynamically managed memory and permanent memory. The SHARED_POOL_SIZE parameter actually specifies the approximate amount of memory in the shared pool available for dynamic allocation, rather than the total size of the shared pool itself.

The permanent shared pool memory contains a variety of data structures such as the buffer headers, the process, session, and transaction arrays, the enqueue resources and locks, the online rollback segment array, and various arrays for recording statistics.

The sizes of most of these arrays are dependent on the settings of one or more initialization parameters. These initialization parameters cannot be changed without shutting down the instance, and so the sizes of the permanent memory arrays are fixed for the life of each instance. For example, the size of the process array is set by the PROCESSES parameter. If all the slots in this array are in use, then any further attempts to create another process in the instance will fail, because the array cannot be dynamically resized.

For many of the permanent memory arrays, there are X$ tables that export each array element as a row, and certain of the structure members as columns. These X$ tables are sometimes called fixed tables. There are also corresponding V$ views that expose the most useful columns of the X$ tables, but only for the rows representing array slots that are currently in use. For example, the V$PROCESS view is based on the X$KSUPR fixed table, which is in turn based on the process array in memory. V$PROCESS does not include all the rows and columns in X$KSUPR, and X$KSUPR does not expose all the members of the SGA process structure.

Learning More About the X$ Tables

People often ask how they can learn more about the X$ tables. My first answer is to say that there is not much of use in the X$ tables that is not also visible in the V$ views. Most of the few useful scraps of information that can be gleaned directly from the X$ tables, but not the V$ views, can be readily obtained using scripts such as those referred to in this book.

But, for those with the passion to know and the hours to burn, the APT script *fixed_table_columns.sql*, which is based on V$FIXED_TABLES, will give you a list of all the X$ tables, their columns, and their data types. You can then use the APT script *fixed_view_text.sql*, which is based on V$FIXED_VIEW_DEFINITION, to get the SQL statement text for all the V$ view definitions. From this information it is easy to work out which X$ tables and which X$ table columns are visible in a V$ view and which are not. Then, working out what extra information the X$ tables contain is a matter of guesswork, trial, and probably some error.

Remember that the X$ tables change significantly from release to release, so scripts should only be based on the X$ tables when it is really necessary.

The size of the variable area of the SGA is equal to the LARGE_POOL_SIZE, plus the SHARED_POOL_SIZE, plus the size of the permanent memory arrays. The total size of the permanent memory arrays can, in theory, be calculated from the settings of the initialization parameters. However, you need to know the formulae used to derive the array sizes from the parameters, the size of each type of array element in bytes, and the sizes of the array headers where applicable. These all change from release to release, and there are also operating system dependent differences. You also need to be aware that each permanent memory array is aligned on a memory page boundary to optimize memory addressing, and so some space is left unused. Fortunately, it is seldom necessary to calculate the permanent memory size precisely. If you really need this information, you can start up a test instance with a dummy SID and measure the permanent memory size, without needing to mount a database.

The database block buffers

This area of the SGA buffers copies of the database blocks. The number of buffers is specified by the DB_BLOCK_BUFFERS parameter, and the size of each buffer is equal to the DB_BLOCK_SIZE for the database. This area of the SGA contains only the buffers themselves, not their control structures. For each buffer there is a corresponding buffer header in the variable area of the SGA. Similarly, the working set headers, the hash chain headers, and their latches reside in the variable area of the SGA. Therefore, you will notice that the size of the variable area of the SGA will change by approximately 1K for every four buffers in the database block buffers area of the SGA.

The log buffer

The size of the log buffer area of the SGA is based on the value specified by the LOG_BUFFER parameter. However, the log buffer will be silently enlarged if an attempt is made to set it to less than its minimum size. The minimum size is four times the maximum database block size supported for the platform. On operating systems that support memory protection, the log buffer is bracketed by two guard pages (or, more correctly, memory protection units) to prevent corruption of the log buffer by errant Oracle processes. Nevertheless, the log buffer area of the SGA should be trivial by comparison with the size of the variable area and the database block buffers. The log buffer is internally divided into blocks. For each log buffer block, there is an 8-byte header in the variable area of the SGA.

The instance lock database

In parallel server configurations, instance locks are used to serialize access to resources that are shared between instances. This area of the SGA maintains a database of the resources in which this instance has an interest, the processes and instances that may need those resources, and the locks currently held or requested by those processes and instances. The sizes of these three arrays are set by the LM_RESS, LM_PROCS, and LM_LOCKS parameters respectively. The instance lock database also includes message buffers and other structures. This area of memory is required even in single-instance Oracle. However, in this case its size is trivial.

This area is not presently included by Oracle when reporting the composition and size of the SGA at instance startup; however, it can be seen in dumps taken with the ORADEBUG IPC command in *svrmgrl*.

Overhead

The last small area of the SGA is the shared memory overhead itself. This area contains information about the shared memory segments in use, and the SGA areas and sub-areas that they contain.

Shared Memory

The SGA resides in shared memory on most operating systems. To understand shared memory segments, you need some understanding of memory segments generally, and thus of virtual memory.

Virtual memory addressing

Today, virtual memory addressing is so prevalent that the alternative of direct memory addressing is almost only a memory. If you once programmed for the Z80 or 8086 CPUs, then you may remember direct memory addressing. You had to know exactly which memory addresses were available to you, so that you did not reference nonexistent memory or corrupt the BIOS. If you needed to write a big program, bigger than the available memory or address space, then you had to break it into sections that could be loaded or switched into memory as required. In fact, the Oracle two-task architecture was initially adopted for this very reason.

Virtual memory addressing introduces a layer of abstraction between program code and physical memory. All memory references are dynamically translated from virtual memory addresses to physical memory addresses before each instruction is executed. The operating system maintains data structures, called page tables, to support virtual-to-physical memory address translation. The most recently used page table entries are cached in each CPU to optimize address translation. This cache is commonly called a translation lookaside buffer (TLB). To further optimize address translation, TLB lookups are performed in hardware. A TLB miss must be resolved by reference to the page tables in main memory. This operation is also performed by hardware in some cases. If hardware address translation fails, the CPU switches into a special execution context to ensure that a physical memory page is allocated for the virtual page and refreshed from disk if necessary. The page table entry is also copied into the TLB. Such hardware address translation failures are called page faults. If a page has to be read from disk, it is called a hard or major page fault—otherwise, it is a soft or minor page fault. After a minor page fault has been resolved, the CPU switches back into user mode and restarts the current instruction. However, while a major page fault is being resolved, the CPU time may be used to service other processes.

Virtual memory addressing enables programs to run when not all of their program code or data is currently in physical memory. This means that relatively inactive virtual pages can be temporarily removed from physical memory if necessary. If these pages have been modified, they must be saved to a temporary storage area on disk, called a paging file or swap space. The operation of writing one or a cluster of inactive memory pages to disk is called a page out, and the corresponding operation of reading them in again later when one of the pages is referenced is called a page in. Paging is the aspect of virtual memory management that allows large programs to run. It is effective because programs typically use only a small proportion of their virtual memory pages actively at any one a time. The set of pages in active use by a process is called its working set.

Virtual memory addressing also enables programs to run from almost any location in physical memory. This means that it is possible to have many programs and their data in memory at the same time, and to switch between them very quickly. CPU time is not wasted while a process performs disk I/O, or waits for user input, or to resolve a page fault.

Memory access

Heavy paging activity can have a major impact on system performance, as is discussed later in this chapter. But first, it's important to note that address translation itself and memory access generally, apart from paging, also affect system performance significantly. Main memory access is expensive in terms of CPU cycles. Memory operates at much lower hardware clock speeds than CPUs do, and there is also a recovery time component required after each memory access before that memory bank can service another memory access by either the same CPU or another one. This is why computer manufacturers put so much effort into their CPU caching technology. Not only are page table entries cached in the TLB, but portions of user memory (called cache lines) are cached in a general cache as well. Sophisticated mechanisms are used to maintain consistency between main memory and the CPU caches (called cache coherency mechanisms). Cache lines are retained as long as possible to maximize cache hits, with a distinction often being made between program code and data because of their different locality properties. At the operating system level, scheduling algorithms are biased towards scheduling processes to get a time slice on the CPU on which they ran most recently. This is intended to minimize the probability of hardware address translation failures and CPU cache misses, and thereby to reduce main memory access.

Your control over memory access performance is limited to purchasing decisions. If you are lucky enough to have a say in such matters, here are the guidelines:

1. Reduce the impact of cache coherency mechanisms by buying fewer, faster CPUs.

2. Further reduce the risk of memory access contention between CPUs by buying a large number of small memory boards.

3. Reduce the cost of memory access for each CPU by buying the fastest available memory. However, if fast memory implies only a few large memory boards, and if you expect to scale beyond six CPUs, then prefer slower memory in more, smaller boards.

4. There are pitfalls associated with mixing different types of memory in the same system. Avoid this, unless your hardware vendor assures you that it is OK.

Process memory segments

One of the benefits of virtual memory addressing is that processes can use a large virtual memory address space regardless of the physical memory available. This enables process memory to be logically divided into distinct segments based on usage. These segments may be mapped to non-contiguous virtual memory addresses to allow for segment growth. Oracle uses the following segment types, as do programs generally:

Program text

The text segment contains the executable machine code for the program itself, excluding dynamically linked shared libraries. Text segments are normally marked read-only, so that they can be shared between multiple processes running the same program. For example, all Oracle processes execute the same *oracle* binary, albeit with different personalities. Regardless of how many processes are running in an instance, and regardless of how many instances are running that release of Oracle on the same server, only one copy of the program text is required in physical memory.

Initialized global data

This segment contains global data structures that are initialized by the compiler, such as text strings for use in trace output. Initialized data can theoretically be modified, and thus it is not shared between processes running the same program. Oracle makes little use of this segment.

Uninitialized global data

The uninitialized data segment is normally called the BSS (Block Started by Symbol) segment. This segment contains statically allocated global data structures that are initialized at runtime by the process itself. Oracle makes minimal use of the BSS segment.

Data heap

The heap is available to processes for the dynamic allocation of memory at runtime using the *malloc()* or *sbrk()* system calls. Oracle uses the heap for its PGA (process global area) which is discussed later in this chapter.

Execution stack

Whenever a function is called, the arguments and the return context are pushed onto the execution stack. The return context is essentially a set of CPU register values that describe the exact state of the process at the point of the function call. When the function call completes, the stack is popped and the context is resumed so that execution continues from the instruction immediately following the function call. The stack also holds variables that are local to a code block. Stack size is dependent on the depth of function call nesting, or recursion, and the memory requirements of the arguments and local variables. Oracle's stack space requirements are modest given its complexity.

Shared libraries

Shared libraries are collections of position-independent executable code implementing functions that may be required by a number of programs—in particular, collections of system call functions. Shared library segments are marked read-only and shared between all dependent processes, including Oracle processes. No more than one copy of each shared library is required in physical memory. Before a function in a shared library can be called, the process must open the shared library file, and map it into its address space using the *mmap()* system call.

The alternative to using shared libraries is to include the required system call functions in the program text segment itself. This is necessary on operating systems that do not support shared libraries, or where the implementation is problematic. On most operating systems,

Oracle uses shared libraries for system call functions but not for the Oracle server code itself. However, Java class libraries are compiled and dynamically linked as shared libraries.

Shared memory segments

Shared memory allows associated processes to cooperatively read and write common data structures in memory. Each process that needs to address a shared memory segment must first attach that segment into its virtual address space. This is normally done using the *shmat()* system call. Oracle uses shared memory segments for the SGA.

The location of these segments in the virtual address space of a process is operating system specific. Some operating systems reserve certain virtual address ranges for particular types of segments. Others allocate the text, data, and BSS segments at the extremities of the virtual address space range, leaving a contiguous unused address space range in between. The stack and heap are allocated at the opposite ends of this range, and grow towards the center. Other segments, such as shared memory segments, must be located between the stack and heap at a location specified by the program itself.

On such operating systems, it is sometimes necessary to control the address at which the SGA is attached, to prevent address range conflicts between the segments. In some cases, this can be done with the SHARED_MEMORY_ADDRESS and HI_SHARED_MEMORY_ADDRESS parameters, but on other systems it is necessary to use *genksms* and modify the attach address in the *ksms.s* file before relinking Oracle. Consult your Oracle installation guide for details.

Intimate shared memory

Each segment in the virtual address space of a process requires page table entries to support virtual-to-physical address translation. If two or more processes have mapped a single memory segment into the same location in their virtual address space, then they can theoretically share the same page table entries. This is called intimate shared memory.

Intimate shared memory boosts Oracle performance in several ways. In particular, it greatly increases the TLB hit rate for page table entries and thus reduces main memory access and speeds up execution significantly. In instances with large shared memory requirements and large numbers of processes, it also results in a significant saving in page table memory—on the order of hundreds of megabytes.

Under some operating systems intimate shared memory is used automatically for Oracle because there is no alternative. In some cases, it is not available because either the operating system or the hardware does not support it. However, in other cases, it is dependent on the _USE_ISM parameter or the size of the shared memory segments.

If _USE_ISM is set to TRUE (the default) on an operating system that supports program-selectable intimate shared memory, then Oracle uses a flag to request intimate shared memory from the operating system for its shared memory segments. However, on some operating systems intimate shared memory is only available for segments for which the page table is itself an exact number of pages in size, and if so it is used automatically. For example, assuming a 32-bit address space and a 4KB memory page size, one page in the page table can address 4MB of memory. In this case shared memory segments must be an exact multiple of 4MB in size if intimate shared memory is to be used. This is always possible to ensure by making small adjustments to the SHARED_POOL_SIZE, DB_BLOCK_BUFFERS, and LOG_BUFFER parameters, and then checking the sizes of the SGA segments using the ORADEBUG IPC command.

A further optimization to address translation is possible on operating systems that allow some segments to use larger than normal memory page sizes. For example, you may be able to use the *chatr* command to request a large page size for the data or instruction segments for a particular executable. Using a large page size reduces the number of page table entries required for each segment, and thus improves the TLB hit rate for the segment, as well as reducing its load on the TLB. Oracle has some built-in dependencies on its memory page size, so check with Oracle Support as to whether it is safe to use a large page size for Oracle on your platform, before attempting to do so.

SGA allocation

When an Oracle instance is started, the sizes of the main SGA areas are first calculated based on the initialization parameters. These are the sizes shown by Oracle when reporting the SGA size. However, before shared memory segments are allocated, the size of each area is rounded up to a memory page boundary.

The areas are then divided into sub-areas, if necessary, so that no sub-area is larger than the operating system limit on the size of a shared memory segment (SHMMAX for System V shared memory under Unix). In the case of the variable area, there is an operating system specific minimum sub-area size, and so the size of the variable area is rounded up further to a multiple of the minimum sub-area size.

Oracle will allocate a single shared memory segment for the entire SGA if possible. However, if the SGA is larger than the operating system limit on the size of a single shared memory segment, then Oracle will use a best fit algorithm to group the sub-areas together into multiple shared memory segments no larger than the maximum size.

Under Oracle7 the variable area of the SGA had to reside in contiguous memory. Therefore, if the operating system did not allow Oracle to specify the virtual memory address at which shared memory segments were to be attached, and thereby to attach them contiguously, then the variable segment had to be small enough to fit in a shared memory segment by itself. This constraint no longer applies in Oracle8, because of the introduction of sub-areas.

It is commonly suggested that the operating system limit on the size of a single shared memory segment should be raised in order to allow Oracle to allocate the SGA in a single shared memory segment if possible. I follow this advice, but only for reasons of manageability. The performance difference is negligible at instance and process startup and is nil otherwise.

Paging

The operating system allocates physical memory pages for the SGA and Oracle processes from its page pool. The page pool comprises all physical system memory excluding that reserved for the operating system itself. A page is allocated from the page pool's free list whenever a virtual memory page that is not in physical memory is referenced. Pages are returned to the head of the free list when memory is deallocated.

If the number of pages on the free list falls below a configurable threshold (LOTSFREE in Unix System V based systems) then the operating system begins to look for inactive pages to page out. Pages are regarded as inactive if they have not been referenced for a certain amount of time. Inactive pages are moved to the end of the free list, but if they have been modified then their contents must first be saved to disk. Paging stops as soon as the number of free pages rises back above the threshold.

If the number of pages on the free list continues to fall, then the operating system steps up the pace of paging by regarding pages as inactive more quickly. However, under extreme memory pressure it is possible for the majority of physical memory to remain very active, so that the operating system searches in vain for sufficient inactive pages. In this case, some low-priority processes will be selected and deactivated entirely to ensure that inactive pages will be able to be found. Although many aspects of this operating system paging behavior are highly tunable, such tuning is seldom beneficial.

Heavy paging activity can have a disastrous effect on system performance. However, high memory usage with intermittent light paging is of no concern. Most systems have plenty of inactive memory that can be paged out with very little performance impact. However, consistent light paging is of some concern because some moderately active pages in the SGA will be paged out repeatedly. Most operating systems provide a mechanism for Oracle to lock the SGA into physical memory to prevent it from paging. If paging is consistent then the LOCK_SGA parameter should be set to TRUE to prevent the SGA from paging. On some operating systems, Oracle needs a special system privilege to be able to use this facility.

How do you determine whether your operating system is paging and, if it is, whether it's paging consistently or heavily? If you have plenty of free memory, then your system will not page at all. If free memory seems scarce, then you can monitor the number of pages paged out per second. This metric is available from the Performance Monitor under NT, or from the *vmstat* command under Unix. If this metric is constantly nonzero, then your system is paging consistently and the SGA should be locked into physical memory if possible. This applies particularly to operating systems with a paged file system buffer cache, such as NT and Solaris.

Note, however, that the page out rate is not a good indication of the intensity of paging activity on operating systems with a paged buffer cache. This is because buffered file system writes are handled by the paging subsystem and thus exaggerate the page out rate. A better indication of the intensity of paging activity on such systems is the scan rate. The scan rate is the number of pages that the operating system has searched per second while looking for inactive pages. The scan rate is reported by *vmstat* on Unix systems under the **sr** column heading. Paging may be regarded as light if the scan rate is below 10 pages per second.

If paging activity is moderate or heavy, then memory pressure must be reduced either by reducing the demand for memory, or by buying more. In particular, beware of oversizing the SGA and then locking it into memory.

The Shared Pool

The part of the SGA that is most commonly oversized is the shared pool. Many DBAs have little understanding of what the shared pool is used for, and how to determine whether it is correctly sized. So they just make it

"BIG!" Sometimes that is not big enough, but more often it is wasteful and can also impair performance.

Chunks

To understand the shared pool better, you need to do little more than take a careful look at X$KSMSP. Each row in this table represents a chunk of shared pool memory. Example 6-2 shows some sample rows.

Example 6-2. Sample Chunks in the Shared Pool

```
SQL> select ksmchcom, ksmchcls, ksmchsiz from x$ksmsp;


KSMCHCOM           KSMCHCLS   KSMCHSIZ
----------------   --------   ----------
KGL handles        recr            496
PL/SQL MPCODE      recr           1624
dictionary cach    freeabl        4256
free memory        free           1088
library cache      freeabl         568
library cache      recr            584
multiblock rea     freeabl        2072
permanent memor    perm        1677104
row cache lru      recr             48
session param v    freeabl        2936
sql area           freeabl        2104
sql area           recr           1208
...
```

When each shared pool chunk is allocated, the code passes a comment to the function that is called to perform the allocation. These comments are visible in the KSMCHCOM column of X$KSMSP, and describe the purpose for which the memory has been allocated.

Each chunk is a little larger than the object it contains because there is a 16-byte header to identify the type, class, and size of the chunk and to contain linked-list pointers used for shared pool management.

There are four main classes of memory chunks. These can be seen in the KSMCHCLS column of X$KSMSP.

free
> Free chunks do not contain a valid object, and are available for allocation without restriction.

recr
> Recreatable chunks contain objects that may be able to be temporarily removed from memory if necessary, and recreated again as required. For example, many of the chunks associated with shared SQL statements are recreatable.

`freeabl`

Freeable chunks contain objects that are normally needed for the duration of a session or call, and are freed thereafter. However, they can sometimes be freed earlier, either in whole or in part. Freeable chunks are not available for temporary removal from memory, because they are not recreatable.

`perm`

Permanent memory chunks contain persistent objects. The large permanent memory chunk may also contain internal free space, which can be released into the shared pool as required.

The APT script called *shared_pool_summary.sql* shows a useful summary of the type, class, and size of all chunks in the shared pool. Example 6-3 is a sample of its output. The total size of the chunks for each type of memory is also visible in the shared pool rows of V$SGASTAT, except that some of the structures in the main permanent memory chunk are also broken out and shown separately.

Example 6-3. Sample Output of shared_pool_summary.sql

```
SQL> @shared_pool_summary
```

KSMCHCOM	CHUNKS	RECR	FREEABL	TOTAL
KGFF heap	6	1296	2528	3824
KGK contexts	2		2400	2400
KGK heap	2	1136		1136
KGL handles	571	178616		178616
KQLS heap	404	87952	524888	612840
PL/SQL DIANA	274	42168	459504	501672
PL/SQL MPCODE	57	14560	88384	102944
PLS cca hp desc	1		168	168
PLS non-lib hp	1	2104		2104
character set m	5		23504	23504
dictionary cach	108		223872	223872
fixed allocatio	9	360		360
free memory	185			614088
kzull	1		48	48
library cache	1612	268312	356312	624624
multiblock rea	1		2072	2072
permanent memor	1			1677104
reserved stoppe	2			48
row cache lru	24	1168		1168
session param v	8		23488	23488
sql area	983	231080	1303792	1534872
table columns	19	18520		18520
table definiti	2	176		176

Free Lists

Free chunks in the shared pool are organized into free lists or buckets, based on their size. The bucket numbers and free chunk sizes are as shown in Table 6-1.

Table 6-1. Free List Buckets and Chunks

Bucket Number	Free Chunk Sizes		
0	Up to 79 bytes		
1	80 bytes	to	143 bytes
2	144 bytes	to	271 bytes
3	272 bytes	to	527 bytes
4	528 bytes	to	1039 bytes
5	1040 bytes	to	2063 bytes
6	2064 bytes	to	4111 bytes
7	4112 bytes	to	8207 bytes
8	8208 bytes	to	16399 bytes
9	16400 bytes	to	32783 bytes
10	32784 bytes and larger		

You may notice that the lower bound on the free chunk sizes for each free list is a binary power plus the 16-byte header. The APT script *shared_pool_free_lists.sql* uses this fact to be able to report the number of chunks and the amount of free space on each free list. Example 6-4 shows some interesting output.

Example 6-4. Sample Output of shared_pool_free_lists.sql

```
SQL> @shared_pool_free_lists

    BUCKET FREE_SPACE FREE_CHUNKS AVERAGE_SIZE    BIGGEST
---------- ---------- ----------- ------------ ----------
         0     166344        3872           42         72
         1      32208         374           86         96
         4        928           1          928        928
         6      11784           4         2946       3328
```

When a process needs a chunk of shared pool memory, it first scans the target free list for the chunk of best fit. If a chunk of exactly the right size is not found, then the scan continues to the end of that free list, looking for the next largest available chunk. If the next largest available chunk is 24 or more bytes larger than required, then that chunk is split and the remaining free space chunk is added to the appropriate free list. If, however, the free list does not contain any chunks of the required size, then the smallest chunk is taken from the next nonempty free list. If all of the remaining free lists are empty, then an LRU chain scan will be attempted, as explained in the next section.

Free list scans, management, and chunk allocations are all performed under the protection of the *shared pool* latch. Clearly, if the shared pool contains a large number of very small free chunks, as illustrated in Example 6-4, then the shared pool latch will be held for a relatively long time when searching these particular free lists. It is, in fact, normal to have a large number of very small free chunks like this, and this is the major cause of contention for the shared pool latch. DBAs often respond to *shared pool* latch contention by increasing the size of the shared pool. Unfortunately, this merely delays the onset of shared pool latch contention, and in the end exacerbates it. Note that from release 8.1.6 there are many more free lists in the shared pool, and thus *shared pool* latch contention is no longer a major problem.

LRU Lists

If a process fails to find a free memory chunk of the required size on the shared pool free lists, then it will attempt to remove chunks containing recreatable objects from the shared pool in order to free a large enough chunk.

There are two categories of recreatable chunks—those that are pinned, and those that are not pinned. The concept of chunks in the shared pool being pinned is often confused with the concept of marking the objects that they contain to be kept using the DBMS_SHARED_POOL.KEEP procedure. Keeping applies only to library cache objects, and is a DBA responsibility. However, all chunks are pinned automatically while the objects that they contain are in use. Recreatable chunks cannot be freed while they are pinned. However, unpinned recreatable chunks can normally be freed.

Unpinned recreatable chunks are organized in the shared pool on two lists, each of which is maintained in LRU (least recently used) order. These are called the transient and recurrent LRU lists. Transient objects are unlikely to be required again, whereas recurrent objects may be. The composition of these lists changes rapidly. Chunks are added to the MRU (most recently used) ends whenever they are unpinned, and they are removed from the lists whenever they are pinned again.

Chunks are also removed from the LRU ends of the lists when a process needs to free shared pool memory for a new allocation. Chunks are flushed in sets of eight chunks alternately—first from the transient list, and then from the recurrent list. Chunks are flushed in LRU order regardless of their size. However, some chunks cannot be flushed. For example, chunks containing library cache objects that have been marked for keeping with

DBMS_SHARED_POOL.KEEP cannot be flushed. These chunks are instead removed from the LRU lists by being pinned.

The length of the transient and recurrent LRU lists of unpinned recreatable chunks can be seen in X$KGHLU, together with the number of chunks that have been flushed, and the number of chunks that have been added to or removed from the LRU lists due to pinning and unpinning. X$KGHLU also shows the number of times that the LRU lists were flushed completely but unsuccessfully, and the size of the most recent such request failure. All these statistics can be checked with the APT script *shared_pool_lru_stats.sql*. See Example 6-5 for sample output.

Example 6-5. Sample Output of shared_pool_lru_stats.sql

```
SQL> @shared_pool_lru_stats
```

RECURRENT CHUNKS	TRANSIENT CHUNKS	FLUSHED CHUNKS	PINS AND RELEASES	ORA-4031 ERRORS	LAST ERROR SIZE
121	164	148447	4126701	0	0

Beware how you interpret these figures, because they are only part of the story. The lengths of the LRU lists and the rate of flushing are both heavily dependent of the memory requirements of the application, and variations in its workload. Neither long nor short LRU lists are necessarily a problem, and the flushing of dead chunks is an important part of healthy memory management. However, based on my experience, if the transient list is more than three times longer than the recurrent list, then the shared pool is probably oversized, and if the ratio of chunk flushes to other LRU operations is more than 1 in 20, then the shared pool is probably too small.

Spare Free Memory

If a large memory request cannot be satisfied either directly from the free lists or from the LRU lists by flushing, then Oracle has one more strategy to try.

Surprisingly, the last resort is not to coalesce contiguous free chunks. When chunks are freed, they may be coalesced with the following chunk, if that chunk is also free. However, Oracle only fully coalesces shared pool free space when the ALTER SYSTEM FLUSH SHARED_POOL command is executed explicitly. So memory allocation requests can and do fail even when the shared pool contains enough contiguous free memory. If that free memory is fragmented into multiple small chunks, then it cannot be used to satisfy large memory allocation requests.

Rather, Oracle's last resort for satisfying large memory allocation requests is to release more memory into the shared pool. Oracle actually keeps aside about half the shared pool memory at instance startup. This memory is then released gradually under memory pressure. Oracle does this to limit fragmentation.

Oracle's spare free memory is concealed in the main permanent memory chunk in the shared pool, together with the fixed tables and other genuine permanent memory structures. This memory is not on the shared pool free lists, and is therefore not available for immediate allocation. It is, however, included in the *free memory* statistic shown in V$SGASTAT.

Chunks of spare free memory are released into the shared pool when necessary. An ORA-4031 error, "unable to allocate x bytes of shared memory," will not be raised for the shared pool until all of this spare free memory has been exhausted.

If an instance still has a fair amount of spare free memory after it has been working at peak load for some time, then that is an indication that the shared pool is considerably larger than necessary. The amount of spare free memory remaining can be checked with the APT script *shared_pool_ spare_free.sql*.

The Reserved List

Since the introduction of paged PL/SQL code in release 7.3, the vast majority of shared pool memory chunks are less than 5000 bytes in size. So much so, that in a mature instance it would be almost futile to search the shared pool free lists and LRU lists for chunks of that size or greater. So, Oracle does not.

Instead, Oracle reserves part of the shared pool for large chunks. The size of this reserved area defaults to 5% of the shared pool, and may be adjusted using the SHARED_POOL_RESERVED_SIZE parameter. As the parameter name indicates, this memory is taken out of the shared pool. The informal term, the reserved pool, should be thought of as a contraction for a longer term, the reserved part of the shared pool. There is just one shared pool, part of which is reserved for large chunks.

Chunks larger than 5000 bytes are placed into the reserved part of the shared pool. This threshold can be set with the _SHARED_POOL_ RESERVED_MIN_ALLOC parameter but should *not* be changed. Small chunks seldom go into the reserved pool, and large chunks seldom go into the rest of the shared pool, except during instance startup.

Free memory in the reserved part of the shared pool is not included on the general shared pool free lists. Instead, a separate reserved free list is maintained. The reserved pool does not, however, have its own LRU lists for unpinned recreatable chunks.

Reserved pool statistics are visible in the V$SHARED_POOL_RESERVED view. In particular, the REQUEST_MISSES column shows the number of times that requests for a large chunk of memory were not able to be satisfied immediately from the reserved free list. This metric should be zero. That is, there should be enough free memory in the reserved part of the shared pool to satisfy short-term demands for freeable memory, without needing to flush unpinned recreatable chunks that would otherwise be cached for the long term.

You can configure your monitoring software to watch the USED_SPACE column of V$SHARED_POOL_RESERVED in an attempt to determine whether the size of the reserved part of the shared pool is appropriate. Alternatively, you can use the APT script *reserved_pool_hwm.sql* to obtain a high-water mark for reserved shared pool usage since instance startup. This script relies upon the fact that, in the absence of reserved list request misses, the first chunk of the reserved list has never been used, and all other chunks have been. Example 6-6 shows some sample output. In many cases you will find that the reserved pool is scarcely used, if at all, and that the default reservation of 5% of the shared pool for large chunks is unduly wasteful. I recommend that you run this script routinely prior to shutdown, and also check the maximum utilization of other resources as shown in V$RESOURCE_LIMIT.

Example 6-6. Sample Output of reserved_pool_hwm.sql

```
SQL> @reserved_pool_hwm

RESERVED_SIZE HIGH_WATER_MARK   USAGE
------------- --------------- -------
       256000           15080      6%
```

Marking Objects for Keeping

In a well-sized shared pool, dead chunks will be flushed out. However, any flushing introduces a risk that valuable objects will be flushed out as well. This applies particularly to recreatable objects that are used only intermittently, but are expensive to recreate, because they are large or require complex processing. You may also not want cached sequences to be flushed out, because this results in the remaining cached sequence numbers never being used.

Of course, the way to mitigate this risk is to mark known valuable objects for keeping in the shared pool using DBMS_SHARED_POOL.KEEP. This procedure loads the object and all subordinate objects into the library cache immediately, and marks them all for keeping. So far as possible, this should be done directly after instance startup to minimize shared pool fragmentation.

It is sometimes mistakenly claimed that large objects such as packages do not have to be marked for keeping, because they will be placed in the reserved part of the shared pool and thus be much less likely to be flushed out. However, most large objects are actually loaded into the shared pool in multiple small chunks, and therefore get no special protection by virtue of their size.

It is also unwise to rely on a high frequency of use to prevent objects from being aged out of the shared pool. If your shared pool is well sized, the LRU lists will be fairly short during periods of peak load, and unpinned objects will age out very quickly, unless they are marked for keeping.

If you don't already have your own scripts to do the job, take a look at APT; it includes a set of scripts that you can use for keeping. The *keep_sys_packages.sql* script keeps some key packages in the SYS schema. You will need to customize this script to include any other SYS packages that may be required by your application. The *keep_cached_sequences.sql* script can be used to mark all cached sequences in the database for keeping. And the *keep_schema.sql* script can be used to mark all candidate objects in your key application schemata for keeping.

Keeping should also be used to protect repeatedly executed cursors, once again, regardless of their size. The APT script *keep_cursors.sql* marks all cursors that have been executed five or more times for keeping.

For completeness, I should also mention that the X$KSMLRU fixed table can also be used to help you identify additional library cache objects that should be kept. X$KSMLRU records statistics about up to ten shared pool chunk allocations that have required flushes. Not all chunk allocations are captured, however. In fact, only the largest candidate allocation is guaranteed to be captured. Another, most unusual aspect of this fixed table is that it is cleared entirely whenever it is queried, so it should not be queried casually.

Flushing the Shared Pool

The only way to coalesce contiguous free chunks in the shared pool is to explicitly flush the shared pool using the ALTER SYSTEM FLUSH SHARED_POOL command. The question of whether you should, or should not do so, tends to divide DBAs.

In practice, flushing the shared pool can relieve *shared pool* latch contention and greatly reduce the risk of ORA-4031 errors, with much less immediate impact on performance than is commonly believed, particularly if key objects have been marked for keeping. On the other hand, if all key objects have been marked for keeping, and if your shared pool is not oversized, then you should scarcely need to flush the shared pool, unless your instance has very demanding, long-term uptime requirements.

My personal preference is to flush the shared pool nightly (after backups) and at other times if shared pool free space is becoming too scarce or too fragmented. However, you may need to ensure that flushing the shared pool does not leave unwanted gaps in cached sequences. This can be done either by marking the sequences for keeping, or, in single-instance Oracle, by temporarily unloading the sequences using the ALTER SEQUENCE NOCACHE command. There are APT scripts to do both. The first has already been mentioned, and the second is called *nice_shared_pool_flush.sql*. The two methods work rather well together. Unloading the sequences does not affect their kept status, but protects them even if they were not kept. Also, using *nice_shared_pool_flush.sql* before instance shutdown prevents sequence number loss even if a SHUTDOWN ABORT is necessary.

Heaps and Subheaps

You may have noticed that the names of the X$ tables for the shared pool begin with either KSM or KGH. These are the names for the Oracle memory manager and heap manager modules, respectively. These two modules work together in very close cooperation. The memory manager is responsible for interfacing with the operating system to obtain memory for use by Oracle, and for static allocations of memory. Dynamic memory management is performed by the heap manager. This is why the shared pool is also called the *SGA heap*.

A heap consists of a heap descriptor and one or more memory extents. A heap can also contain subheaps. In this case, the heap descriptor and extents of the subheap are seen as chunks in the parent heap. Heap descriptors vary in size depending on the type of heap and contain list headers for the heap's free lists and LRU lists. An extent has a small header for pointers to the previous and next extents, and the rest of its memory is available to the heap for dynamic allocation.

Except for the reserved list feature, subheaps within the shared pool have exactly the same structure as the shared pool itself. Memory is allocated in chunks. Free chunks are organized on free lists according to size. And unpinned recreatable chunks are maintained on two LRU lists for recurrent and transient chunks, respectively. Subheaps even have a main permanent memory chunk that may contain spare free memory. Subheaps may also contain further subheaps, up to a nesting depth of four.

The concept of subheaps is important to understand because most of the objects that are cached in the shared pool actually reside in subheaps, rather than in the top-level heap itself. Finding space for a new chunk within a subheap is much like finding space for a new chunk within the shared pool itself, except that subheaps can grow by allocating a new extent, whereas the shared pool has a fixed number of extents. The allocation of new extents for subheaps is governed by a minimum extent size, so it is possible to search for a small chunk in a subheap and fail, because none of the parent heaps could allocate a chunk of the required minimum extent sizes.

The Large Pool

If the LARGE_POOL_SIZE parameter is set, then the large pool is configured as a separate heap within the variable area of the SGA. The large pool is not part of the shared pool, and is protected by the *large memory latch*. The large pool only contains free and freeable chunks. It does not contain any recreatable chunks, and so the heap manager's LRU mechanism is not used.

To prevent fragmentation of the large pool, all large pool chunks are rounded up to _LARGE_POOL_MIN_ALLOC, which defaults to 16K. This parameter should not be tuned. It does not affect whether or not certain chunks will be allocated in the large pool. Rather, if a large pool is configured, chunks are allocated explicitly in the large pool based on their usage, and rounded up to the required size if necessary.

It is recommended that you configure a large pool if you use any of the following Oracle features:

• Multi-Threaded Server (MTS) or Oracle*XA

• Recovery Manager (RMAN)

• Parallel Execution (PX)—formerly Parallel Query Option (PQO)

Process Memory

In addition to the SGA, or System Global Area, each Oracle process uses three similar global areas as well:

- The Process Global Area (PGA)
- The User Global Area (UGA)
- The Call Global Area (CGA)

Many DBAs are unclear about the distinction between the PGA and the UGA. The distinction is as simple as that between a process and a session. Although there is commonly a one-to-one relationship between processes and sessions, it can be more complex than that. The most obvious case is a Multi-Threaded Server configuration, in which there can be many more sessions than processes. In such configurations there is one PGA for each process, and one UGA for each session. The PGA contains information that is independent of the session that the process may be serving at any one time, whereas the UGA contains information that is specific to a particular session.

The PGA

The Process Global Area, often known as the Program Global Area, resides in process private memory, rather than in shared memory. It is a global area in the sense that it contains global variables and data structures that must be accessible to all modules of the Oracle server code. However, it is not shared between processes. Each Oracle server process has its own PGA, which contains only process-specific information. Structures in the PGA do not need to be protected by latches because no other process can access them.

The PGA contains information about the operating system resources that the process is using, and some information about the state of the process. However, information about shared Oracle resources that the process is using resides in the SGA. This is necessary so those resources can be cleaned up and freed in the event of the unexpected death of the process.

The PGA consists of two component areas, the fixed PGA and the variable PGA, or PGA heap. The fixed PGA serves a similar purpose to the fixed SGA. It is fixed in size, and contains several hundred atomic variables, small data structures, and pointers into the variable PGA.

The variable PGA is a heap. Its chunks are visible to the process in X$KSMPP, which has the same structure as X$KSMSP. The PGA heap contains permanent memory for a number of fixed tables, which are

dependent on certain parameter settings. These include DB_FILES, LOG_
FILES (prior to release 8.1), and CONTROL_FILES. Beyond that, the PGA
heap is almost entirely dedicated to its subheaps, mainly the UGA (if
applicable) and the CGA.

The UGA

The User Global Area contains information that is specific to a particular
session, including:

- The persistent and runtime areas for open cursors

- State information for packages, in particular package variables

- Java session state

- The roles that are enabled

- Any trace events that are enabled

- The NLS parameters that are in effect

- Any database links that are open

- The session's mandatory access control (MAC) label for Trusted Oracle

Like the PGA, the UGA also consists of two component areas, the fixed
UGA and the variable UGA, or UGA heap. The fixed UGA contains about
70 atomic variables, small data structures, and pointers into the UGA heap.

The chunks in the UGA heap are visible to its session in X$KSMUP, which
has the same structure as X$KSMSP. The UGA heap contains permanent
memory for a number of fixed tables, which are dependent on certain
parameter settings. These include OPEN_CURSORS, OPEN_LINKS, and
MAX_ENABLED_ROLES. Beyond that, the UGA heap is largely dedicated
to private SQL and PL/SQL areas.

The location of the UGA in memory depends on the session configuration. In dedicated server connections where there is a permanent one-to-
one relationship between a session and a process, the UGA is located
within the PGA. The fixed UGA is a chunk within the PGA, and the UGA
heap is a subheap of the PGA. In Multi-Threaded Server and XA connections, the fixed UGA is a chunk within the shared pool, and the UGA
heap is a subheap of the large pool or, failing that, the shared pool.

In configurations in which the UGA is located in the SGA, it may be
prudent to constrain the amount of SGA memory that each user's UGA can
consume. This can be done using the PRIVATE_SGA profile resource limit.

The CGA

Unlike the other global areas, the Call Global Area is transient. It only exists for the duration of a call. A CGA is required for most low-level calls to the instance, including calls to:

- Parse an SQL statement
- Execute an SQL statement
- Fetch the outputs of a SELECT statement

A separate CGA is required for recursive calls. Recursive calls to query data dictionary information may be required during statement parsing, to check the semantics of a statement, and during statement optimization to evaluate alternative execution plans. Recursive calls are also needed during the execution of PL/SQL blocks to process the component SQL statements, and during DML statement execution to process trigger execution.

The CGA is a subheap of the PGA, regardless of whether the UGA is located in the PGA or SGA. An important corollary of this fact is that sessions are bound to a process for the duration of any call. This is particularly important to understand when developing applications for Oracle's Multi-Threaded Server. If some calls are protracted, the number of processes configured must be increased to compensate for that.

Of course, calls do not work exclusively with data structures in their CGA. In fact, the most important data structures involved in calls are typically in the UGA. For example, private SQL and PL/SQL areas and sort areas must be in the UGA because they must persist between calls. The CGA only contains data structures that can be freed at the end of the call. For example, the CGA contains direct I/O buffers, information about recursive calls, stack space for expression evaluation, and other temporary data structures.

Java call memory is also allocated in the CGA. This memory is managed more intensively than any other Oracle memory region. It is divided into three spaces, the stack space, the new space, and the old space. Chunks within the new space and old space that are no longer referenced are garbage collected during call execution with varying frequency based on their length of tenure and size. New space chunks are copied to the old space once they have survived a certain number of new space garbage collection iterations. This is the only garbage collection in Oracle's memory management. All other Oracle memory management relies on the explicit freeing of dead chunks.

Process Memory Allocation

Unlike the SGA, which is fixed in size at instance startup, the PGA can and does grow. It grows by using the *malloc()* or *sbrk()* system calls to extend the heap data segment for the process. The new operating system virtual memory is then added to the PGA heap as a new extent. These extents are normally only a few kilobytes in size, and Oracle may well allocate thousands of them if necessary.

There are, however, operating system limits on the growth of the heap data segment of a process. In most cases the default limit is set by an operating system kernel parameter (commonly MAXDSIZ). In some cases that default can be changed on a per-process basis. There is also a system-wide limit on the total virtual memory size of all processes. That limit is related to the amount of swap space* available. If either of these limits is exceeded, then the Oracle process concerned will return an ORA-4030 error.

This error is only rarely due to the per-process resource limit, and normally indicates a shortage of swap space. To diagnose the problem, you can use the operating system facility to report swap space usage. Alternatively, on some operating systems Oracle includes a small utility called *maxmem* which can be used to check the maximum heap data segment size that a process can allocate, and which limit is being hit first.

If the problem is a shortage of swap space, and if paging activity is moderate or heavy, then you should attempt to reduce the system-wide virtual memory usage either by reducing the process count or by reducing the per-process memory usage. Otherwise, if paging activity is light or nil, you should increase the swap space or, preferably, if your operating system supports it, you should enable the use of virtual or pseudo swap space.

This operating system facility allows system-wide total virtual memory to exceed swap space by approximately the amount of physical memory that is not locked. Some system administrators are unreasonably opposed to the use of this feature in the mistaken belief that it causes paging to memory. It does not. It does, however, significantly reduce the amount of swap space required on large memory systems. Incidentally, the truism that swap space should exceed physical memory by a factor of at least two is not true. It depends on the operating system, memory size, and memory usage, but many systems need virtually no swap space at all.

---

* Please read *paging file space* for *swap space* in this discussion, if that is the correct term on your operating system.

Process Memory Deallocation

Oracle heaps grow much more readily than they shrink, but contrary to popular belief they can and do shrink. The session statistics *session uga memory* and *session pga memory* visible in V$MYSTAT and V$SESSTAT show the current size of the UGA and PGA heaps respectively, including internal free space. The corresponding statistics *session uga memory max* and *session pga memory max* show the peak size of the respective heaps during the life of the session.

The UGA and PGA heaps only shrink after certain operations, such as the merge phase of a disk sort, or when the user explicitly attempts to free memory using the DBMS_SESSION.FREE_UNUSED_USER_MEMORY procedure. However, only entirely free heap extents are released to the parent heap or to the process data heap segment. So some internal free space remains, even after memory has been explicitly freed.

Although it is technically possible to do so, on most operating systems Oracle does not attempt to reduce the size of the process data heap segment and release that virtual memory back to the operating system. So from an operating system point of view, the virtual memory size of an Oracle process remains at its high-water mark. Oracle relies on the operating system to page out any unused virtual pages if necessary. For this reason, operating system statistics about the virtual memory sizes of Oracle processes should be regarded as misleading. The internal Oracle statistics should be used instead, and even these tend to overstate the true memory requirements.

The DBMS_SESSION.FREE_UNUSED_USER_MEMORY procedure need only be used in Multi-Threaded Server applications. It should be used sparingly and only to release the memory used by large package array variables back to the large pool or shared pool. However, that memory must first be freed within the UGA heap, either by assigning an empty array to the array variable, or by calling the DBMS_SESSION.RESET_ PACKAGE procedure.

Please disregard the comments in the DBMS_SESSION package specification to the effect that memory, once used for a purpose, can only ever be reused for the same purpose, and that it is necessary to free unused user memory after a large sort. What is intended is that memory, once allocated to a subheap, is normally only available within that subheap, until the entire subheap has been freed. However, many subheaps, such as the CGA, are freed so quickly that the statement is, at best, misleading. Moreover, it is not normally necessary to free unused user memory after a sort, not even in Multi-Threaded Server applications, because the majority of sort memory is, in fact, freed automatically.

Taking Heapdumps

Oracle Support may sometimes ask you to take heapdumps to help to diagnose a potential memory problem. Heapdumps may be taken in the current process using the ALTER SESSION SET EVENTS command, or in another session using the ORADEBUG EVENT command. Heapdumps are written to a trace file in the process's dump destination directory, and contain largely the same information as the corresponding X$ tables.

The event syntax for heapdumps of the primary heaps is IMMEDIATE TRACE NAME HEAPDUMP LEVEL *n*. The level number is a bit pattern representing which heaps should be dumped: 1 for the PGA, 2 for the SGA, 4 for the UGA, 8 for the CGA, and 32 for the large pool.

The event syntax for heapdumps of arbitrary subheaps is IMMEDIATE TRACE NAME HEAPDUMP_ADDR LEVEL *n*, where *n* is the decimal equivalent of the hexadecimal address of the heap descriptor. Subheap heap descriptor addresses are visible in the KSMCHPAR column of the KSM X$ tables, and in heapdumps of their parent heaps alongside the ds= string.

Reference

This section contains a quick reference to the parameters, events, statistics, and APT scripts mentioned in Chapter 6.

Parameters

Parameter	Description
_LARGE_POOL_MIN_ALLOC	Large pool chunk allocations are rounded up to this size. This parameter defaults to 16K, and should not be changed.
_USE_ISM	Intimate shared memory is used by default where possible. However, the implementation is problematic on some operating systems, and so it is sometimes necessary to set this parameter to FALSE.
DB_BLOCK_BUFFERS DB_BLOCK_SIZE	The product of these two parameters dictates the size of the SGA area for the database block buffers.

Parameter	Description
DB_FILES LOG_FILES (prior to 8.1) CONTROL_FILES	These parameters affect the size of the fixed PGA. They should not be any larger than reasonably necessary.
LARGE_POOL_SIZE	Certain demands for large chunks of memory are satisfied from the large pool, if a large pool has been configured. This parameter sets the size of the large pool in bytes.
LOCK_SGA	If operating system paging is consistent, this parameter should be set to TRUE, to prevent the SGA from paging.
LOG_BUFFER	Although the log buffer has a separate area in the SGA, it should nevertheless be trivial in size.
OPEN_CURSORS OPEN_LINKS MAX_ENABLED_ROLES	These parameters affect the size of the fixed UGA. They should not be any larger than necessary.
PRE_PAGE_SGA	If set to TRUE, this causes all Oracle server processes to page in the entire SGA on process startup if necessary. This may yield a marginal improvement in performance during the period shortly after instance startup, but only at the considerable cost of slowing down all process startups.
SESSIONS	This is the parameter that has the greatest effect on the total size of the fixed tables in the permanent memory chunk of the shared pool.
SHARED_MEMORY_ADDRESS HI_SHARED_MEMORY_ ADDRESS	On some platforms, these parameters may be used to specify the virtual memory address at which the SGA should be attached.
SHARED_POOL_RESERVED_SIZE	Shared pool chunk allocations larger than 5000 bytes are satisfied from the shared pool reserved list. This parameter sets the size of the reserved list in bytes. The threshold size for reserved list allocation, which is set by the _SHARED_POOL_RESERVED_MIN_ALLOC parameter, should not be changed.
SHARED_POOL_SIZE	This parameter sets the approximate amount of memory in the shared pool available for dynamic allocation, expressed in bytes.
SORT_AREA_SIZE	This parameter can have a big impact on memory usage and performance.

Events

Event	Description
4030	This is the out of process memory error event. To take PGA, UGA, and CGA heapdumps at the exact time of this error, set the following event in your parameter file: `event = "4030 trace name heapdump level 13"`
4031	This is the out of shared memory error event. If you are struggling with repeated ORA-4031 errors, you may wish to take an SGA heapdump at the exact time of the error by setting the following event in your parameter file: `event = "4031 trace name heapdump level 2"` In Multi-Threaded Server environments, you may wish to use level 6 instead, to include a UGA heapdump as well.
10235	This event causes the Oracle server code to continually check the integrity of the memory and heap management data structures. This is sometimes necessary to diagnose suspected memory corruption issues. Unfortunately, this event can only be set instance-wide. It cannot be set on a single process. Only set this event under direction from Oracle Support, and then only as a last resort. Even the minimal checking at level 1 has a *severe* impact on performance.

Statistics

Statistic	Source	Description
free memory	V$SGASTAT	Free memory in the SGA heap. This includes chunks on the free lists and spare free memory in the permanent memory chunk, but does not include unpinned recreatable chunks.
session uga memory	V$MYSTAT and V$SESSTAT	The current size of the UGA heap for the session, excluding the fixed UGA.
session uga memory max	V$MYSTAT and V$SESSTAT	The UGA heap size high-water mark.
session pga memory	V$MYSTAT and V$SESSTAT	The current size of the PGA heap for the session, excluding the fixed PGA.
session pga memory max	V$MYSTAT and V$SESSTAT	The PGA heap size high-water mark.

APT Scripts

Script	Description
fixed_table_columns.sql	Gets a description of all the X$ tables.
fixed_view_text.sql	Extracts the SQL statement text for all the V$ views.
keep_cached_sequences.sql	Marks all cached sequences for keeping in the shared pool.
keep_cursors.sql	Marks cursors that have been executed five or more times for keeping in the shared pool.
keep_schema.sql	Marks all candidate objects in an application schema for keeping in the shared pool.
keep_sys_packages.sql	Marks some key packages in the SYS schema for keeping.
nice_shared_pool_flush.sql	Flushes the shared pool, but unloads all cached sequences first, to prevent gaps lest they were not kept.
reserved_pool_hwm.sql	Shows the high-water mark usage of the reserved pool. This can be used to check whether the reserved pool is too large.
shared_pool_free_lists.sql	Shows the composition of the shared pool free lists.
shared_pool_lru_stats.sql	Shows key statistics for the shared pool LRU lists.
shared_pool_spare_free.sql	Shows how spare free memory remains in the shared pool.
shared_pool_summary.sql	Shows a summary of the shared pool by chunk usage, class, and size.

Index

About the Author

Steve Adams runs a small consulting company, Ixora, that specializes in advanced Unix and Oracle performance tuning. He is based in Sydney, Australia, but also works remotely for clients in America and Europe. Steve is a regular contributor to various Oracle discussion forums on the Internet, where he is widely regarded as the leading performance expert. His experience with Oracle dates back to version 3 (1984). However, most of his work has been in Unix performance tuning. His interest in Oracle—and Oracle internals in particular—was rekindled when working as the Unix performance expert on a benchmark of an Oracle-based application in 1995. He found the challenge of understanding Oracle performance to be extremely demanding, and yet irresistible. Steve doesn't yet claim to have mastered the topic of Oracle performance, but he does have plenty of insight to share. He can be contacted directly at *steve.adams@ixora.com.au* or via his company's web site at *http://www.ixora.com.au/*.

Colophon

Our look is the result of reader comments, our own experimentation, and feedback from distribution channels. Distinctive covers complement our distinctive approach to technical topics, breathing personality and life into potentially dry subjects.

The animal on the cover of *Oracle 8i Internal Services* is a bumblebee. Only three types of bees are social insects: bumblebees, honeybees, and tropical stingless bees. There are approximately 200 species of bumblebee, most of which reside in temperate zones, where their thick layer of hair protects them from cool temperatures. In early spring the queen bee emerges from underground hibernation and searches for a nesting site, often in a deserted rodent nest. She then makes a honey pot of secreted wax, and a cell into which she places pollen and lays the first of her eggs. When these eggs hatch, the larvae grow into small worker bees. Later broods of eggs grow into bigger bees, as the queen now has help gathering food for the larvae. Toward the end of the breeding season, males and young queens are produced. By late autumn, the entire colony has died, with the exception of the young queens, who scatter to find places to hibernate until the following spring, when they will begin their own colonies.

The disproportionate appearance of bumblebees is deceptive. Despite their large, apparently clumsy bodies and delicate wings, they move swiftly and efficiently, pollinating flowers as they go. Bumblebees play an important role in pollinating flowers such as the red clover, in which the nectar is too deep down for most bees to reach. This is because the bumblebee's tongue is, on average, 2.5 mm longer than other that of other bees. In New Zealand, English settlers discovered that the red clover that they transported and planted did not thrive until they imported bumblebees to aid with pollination.

Colleen Gorman was the production editor and proofreader for *Oracle 8i Internal Services*; Nicole Gipson Arigo and Jeff Holcomb provided quality control. Mike Sierra provided FrameMaker technical support. Steve Adams wrote the index.

Ellie Volckhausen designed the cover of this book, using an original drawing by Lorrie LeJeune. Kathleen Wilson produced the cover layout using Quark-XPress 3.3 and the ITC Garamond font. Whenever possible, our books use RepKover™, a durable and flexible lay-flat binding. If the page count exceeds RepKover's limit, perfect binding is used.

Alicia Cech designed the interior layout based on a series design by Nancy Priest. It was implemented in FrameMaker 5.5 by Mike Sierra. The text and heading fonts are ITC Garamond Light and Garamond Book. The illustrations that appear in the book were produced by Robert Romano and Rhon Porter using Macromedia FreeHand 8 and Adobe Photoshop 5. This colophon was written by Clairemarie Fisher O'Leary.

More Titles from O'Reilly

Oracle

Advanced Oracle PL/SQL Programming with Packages

By Steven Feuerstein
1st Edition October 1996
690 pages, Includes diskette
ISBN 1-56592-238-7

This book explains the best way to construct packages, a powerful part of Oracle's PL/SQL procedural language that can dramatically improve your programming productivity and code quality, while preparing you for object-oriented development in Oracle technology. It comes with PL/Vision software, a library of PL/SQL packages developed by the author, and takes you behind the scenes as it examines how and why the PL/Vision packages were implemented the way they were.

Oracle Design

By Dave Ensor & Ian Stevenson
1st Edition March 1997
546 pages, ISBN 1-56592-268-9

This book looks thoroughly at the field of Oracle relational database design, an often neglected area of Oracle, but one that has an enormous impact on the ultimate power and performance of a system. Focuses on both database and code design, including such special design areas as data models, denormalization, the use of keys and indexes, temporal data, special architectures (client/server, distributed database, parallel processing), and data warehouses.

Oracle Built-in Packages

By Steven Feuerstein,
Charles Dye & John Beresniewicz
1st Edition April 1998
956 pages, Includes diskette
ISBN 1-56592-375-8

Oracle's built-in packages dramatically extend the power of the PL/SQL language, but few developers know how to use them effectively. This book is a complete reference to all of the built-ins, including those new to Oracle8. The enclosed diskette includes an online tool that provides easy access to the many files of source code and documentation developed by the authors.

Oracle Web Applications: PL/SQL Developer's Introduction

By Andrew Odewahn
1st Edition September 1999 (est.)
264 pages (est.), ISBN 1-56592-687-0

This book is an easy-to-understand guide to building Oracle8i (Oracle's "Internet database") Web applications using a variety of tools – PL/SQL, HTML, XML, WebDB, and Oracle Application Server (OAS). It also covers the packages in the PL/SQL toolkit and demonstrates several fully realized Web applications. This book provides the jump-start you need to extend relational concepts to Web content and to make the transition from traditional programming to the development of useful Web applications for Oracle8i. Also covers Web development for Oracle8 and Oracle7.

Oracle SQL*Plus: The Definitive Guide

By Jonathan Gennick
1st Edition March 1999
526 pages, ISBN 1-56592-578-5

This book is the definitive guide to SQL*Plus, Oracle's interactive query tool. Despite the wide availability and usage of SQL*Plus, few developers and DBAs know how powerful it really is. This book introduces SQL*Plus, provides a syntax quick reference, and describes how to write and execute script files, generate ad hoc reports, extract data from the database, query the data dictionary tables, use the SQL*Plus administrative features (new in Oracle8i), and much more.

Oracle PL/SQL Programming, 2nd Edition

By Steven Feuerstein with Bill Pribyl
2nd Edition September 1997
1028 pages, Includes diskette
ISBN 1-56592-335-9

The first edition of *Oracle PL/SQL Programming* quickly became an indispensable reference for PL/SQL developers. The second edition focuses on Oracle8, covering Oracle8 object types, object views, collections, and external procedures, as well as new datatypes and functions and tuning, tracing, and debugging PL/SQL programs. The diskette contains an online Windows-based tool with access to more than 100 files of source code.

O'REILLY®

TO ORDER: **800-998-9938** • *order@oreilly.com* • *http://www.oreilly.com/*

OUR PRODUCTS ARE AVAILABLE AT A BOOKSTORE OR SOFTWARE STORE NEAR YOU.

FOR INFORMATION: **800-998-9938** • **707-829-0515** • *info@oreilly.com*

Oracle

Oracle Performance Tuning, 2nd Edition

By Mark Gurry & Peter Corrigan
2nd Edition November 1996
964 pages, Includes diskette
ISBN 1-56592-237-9

The first edition of this book became a classic for developers and DBAs. This edition offers 400 pages of updated material on Oracle features, including parallel server, parallel query, Oracle Performance Pack, disk striping and mirroring, RAID, MPPs, SMPs, distributed databases, backup and recovery, and much more. Includes a diskette containing the SQL and shell scripts described in the book.

Oracle Distributed Systems

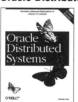

By Charles Dye
1st Edition April 1999
548 pages, Includes diskette
ISBN 1-56592-432-0

This book describes how you can use multiple databases and both Oracle8 and Oracle7 distributed system features to best advantage. It covers design, configuration of SQL*Net/Net8, security, and Oracle's distributed options (advanced replication, snapshots, multi-master replication, updateable snapshots, procedural replication, and conflict resolution). Includes a complete API reference for built-in packages and a diskette many helpful scripts and utilities.

Oracle Scripts

By Brian Lomasky & David C. Kreines
1st Edition May 1998
204 pages, Includes CD-ROM
ISBN 1-56592-438-X

A powerful toolset for Oracle DBAs and developers, these scripts will simplify everyday tasks – monitoring databases, protecting against data loss, improving security and performance, and helping to diagnose problems and repair databases in emergencies. The accompanying CD-ROM contains complete source code and additional monitoring and tuning software.

Oracle Security

By Marlene Theriault & William Heney
1st Edition October 1998
446 pages, ISBN 1-56592-450-9

This book covers the field of Oracle security from simple to complex. It describes basic RDBMS security features (e.g., passwords, profiles, roles, privileges, synonyms) and includes many practical strategies for securing an Oracle system, developing auditing and backup plans, and using the Oracle Enterprise Manager and Oracle Security Server. Also touches on advanced security features, such as encryption, Trusted Oracle, and Internet and Web protection.

Oracle Database Administration: The Essential Reference

By David Kreines & Brian Laskey
1st Edition April 1999
580 pages, ISBN 1-56592-516-5

This book provides a concise reference to the enormous store of information Oracle8 or Oracle7 DBAs need every day. It covers DBA tasks (e.g., installation, tuning, backups, networking, auditing, query optimization) and provides quick references to initialization parameters, SQL statements, data dictionary tables, system privileges, roles, and syntax for SQL*Plus, Export, Import, and SQL*Loader.

Oracle SAP Administration

By Donald K. Burleson
1st Edition September 1999 (est.)
200 pages (est.), ISBN 1-56592-696-X

This book provides tried-and-true advice for administrators and developers who use the SAP business system and the Oracle database system (Oracle8 or Oracle7) in combination. It covers SAP's SAPDBA and SAPGUI utilities and describes effective data file placement, initialization parameters, and monitoring techniques, as well as high-performance table reorganization, backup, recovery, tuning, and parallel processing.

How to stay in touch with O'Reilly

1. Visit Our Award-Winning Site

http://www.oreilly.com/

★ "Top 100 Sites on the Web" —*PC Magazine*
★ "Top 5% Web sites" —*Point Communications*
★ "3-Star site" —*The McKinley Group*

Our web site contains a library of comprehensive product information (including book excerpts and tables of contents), downloadable software, background articles, interviews with technology leaders, links to relevant sites, book cover art, and more. File us in your Bookmarks or Hotlist!

2. Join Our Email Mailing Lists

New Product Releases
To receive automatic email with brief descriptions of all new O'Reilly products as they are released, send email to:
listproc@online.oreilly.com
Put the following information in the first line of your message (*not* in the Subject field):
subscribe oreilly-news

O'Reilly Events
If you'd also like us to send information about trade show events, special promotions, and other O'Reilly events, send email to:
listproc@online.oreilly.com
Put the following information in the first line of your message (*not* in the Subject field):
subscribe oreilly-events

3. Get Examples from Our Books via FTP

There are two ways to access an archive of example files from our books:

Regular FTP
- ftp to:
  ftp.oreilly.com
  (login: anonymous
  password: your email address)
- Point your web browser to:
  ftp://ftp.oreilly.com/

FTPMAIL
- Send an email message to:
  ftpmail@online.oreilly.com
  (Write "help" in the message body)

4. Contact Us via Email

order@oreilly.com
To place a book or software order online. Good for North American and international customers.

subscriptions@oreilly.com
To place an order for any of our newsletters or periodicals.

books@oreilly.com
General questions about any of our books.

software@oreilly.com
For general questions and product information about our software. Check out O'Reilly Software Online at **http://software.oreilly.com/** for software and technical support information. Registered O'Reilly software users send your questions to:
website-support@oreilly.com

cs@oreilly.com
For answers to problems regarding your order or our products.

booktech@oreilly.com
For book content technical questions or corrections.

proposals@oreilly.com
To submit new book or software proposals to our editors and product managers.

international@oreilly.com
For information about our international distributors or translation queries. For a list of our distributors outside of North America check out:
http://www.oreilly.com/www/order/country.html

O'Reilly & Associates, Inc.
101 Morris Street, Sebastopol, CA 95472 USA
TEL   707-829-0515 or 800-998-9938
          (6am to 5pm PST)
FAX   707-829-0104

O'REILLY®

International Distributors

UK, EUROPE, MIDDLE EAST AND AFRICA (EXCEPT FRANCE, GERMANY, AUSTRIA, SWITZERLAND, LUXEMBOURG, LIECHTENSTEIN, AND EASTERN EUROPE)

INQUIRIES
O'Reilly UK Limited
4 Castle Street
Farnham
Surrey, GU9 7HS
United Kingdom
Telephone: 44-1252-711776
Fax: 44-1252-734211
Email: josette@oreilly.com

ORDERS
Wiley Distribution Services Ltd.
1 Oldlands Way
Bognor Regis
West Sussex PO22 9SA
United Kingdom
Telephone: 44-1243-779777
Fax: 44-1243-820250
Email: cs-books@wiley.co.uk

FRANCE
ORDERS
GEODIF
61, Bd Saint-Germain
75240 Paris Cedex 05, France
Tel: 33-1-44-41-46-16 (French books)
Tel: 33-1-44-41-11-87 (English books)
Fax: 33-1-44-41-11-44
Email: distribution@eyrolles.com

INQUIRIES
Éditions O'Reilly
18 rue Séguier
75006 Paris, France
Tel: 33-1-40-51-52-30
Fax: 33-1-40-51-52-31
Email: france@editions-oreilly.fr

GERMANY, SWITZERLAND, AUSTRIA, EASTERN EUROPE, LUXEMBOURG, AND LIECHTENSTEIN

INQUIRIES & ORDERS
O'Reilly Verlag
Balthasarstr. 81
D-50670 Köln
Germany
Telephone: 49-221-973160-91
Fax: 49-221-973160-8
Email: anfragen@oreilly.de (inquiries)
Email: order@oreilly.de (orders)

CANADA (FRENCH LANGUAGE BOOKS)
Les Éditions Flammarion ltée
375, Avenue Laurier Ouest
Montréal (Québec) H2V 2K3
Tel: 00-1-514-277-8807
Fax: 00-1-514-278-2085
Email: info@flammarion.qc.ca

HONG KONG
City Discount Subscription Service, Ltd.
Unit D, 3rd Floor, Yan's Tower
27 Wong Chuk Hang Road
Aberdeen, Hong Kong
Tel: 852-2580-3539
Fax: 852-2580-6463
Email: citydis@ppn.com.hk

KOREA
Hanbit Media, Inc.
Sonyoung Bldg. 202
Yeksam-dong 736-36
Kangnam-ku
Seoul, Korea
Tel: 822-554-9610
Fax: 822-556-0363
Email: hant93@chollian.dacom.co.kr

PHILIPPINES
Mutual Books, Inc.
429-D Shaw Boulevard
Mandaluyong City, Metro
Manila, Philippines
Tel: 632-725-7538
Fax: 632-721-3056
Email: mbikikog@mnl.sequel.net

TAIWAN
O'Reilly Taiwan
No. 3, Lane 131
Hang-Chow South Road
Section 1, Taipei, Taiwan
Tel: 886-2-23968990
Fax: 886-2-23968916
Email: taiwan@oreilly.com

CHINA
O'Reilly Beijing
Room 2410
160, FuXingMenNeiDaJie
XiCheng District
Beijing
China PR 100031
Tel: 86-10-86631006
Fax: 86-10-86631007
Email: beijing@oreilly.com

INDIA
Computer Bookshop (India) Pvt. Ltd.
190 Dr. D.N. Road, Fort
Bombay 400 001 India
Tel: 91-22-207-0989
Fax: 91-22-262-3551
Email: cbsbom@giasbm01.vsnl.net.in

JAPAN
O'Reilly Japan, Inc.
Kiyoshige Building 2F
12-Bancho, Sanei-cho
Shinjuku-ku
Tokyo 160-0008 Japan
Tel: 81-3-3356-5227
Fax: 81-3-3356-5261
Email: japan@oreilly.com

ALL OTHER ASIAN COUNTRIES
O'Reilly & Associates, Inc.
101 Morris Street
Sebastopol, CA 95472 USA
Tel: 707-829-0515
Fax: 707-829-0104
Email: order@oreilly.com

AUSTRALIA
WoodsLane Pty., Ltd.
7/5 Vuko Place
Warriewood NSW 2102
Australia
Tel: 61-2-9970-5111
Fax: 61-2-9970-5002
Email: info@woodslane.com.au

NEW ZEALAND
Woodslane New Zealand, Ltd.
21 Cooks Street (P.O. Box 575)
Waganui, New Zealand
Tel: 64-6-347-6543
Fax: 64-6-345-4840
Email: info@woodslane.com.au

LATIN AMERICA
McGraw-Hill Interamericana
Editores, S.A. de C.V.
Cedro No. 512
Col. Atlampa
06450, Mexico, D.F.
Tel: 52-5-547-6777
Fax: 52-5-547-3336
Email: mcgraw-hill@infosel.net.mx

O'REILLY®

TO ORDER: **800-998-9938** • **order@oreilly.com** • **http://www.oreilly.com/**
OUR PRODUCTS ARE AVAILABLE AT A BOOKSTORE OR SOFTWARE STORE NEAR YOU.
FOR INFORMATION: **800-998-9938** • **707-829-0515** • **info@oreilly.com**

O'REILLY WOULD LIKE TO HEAR FROM YOU

Which book did this card come from?

_____

Where did you buy this book?
- ❏ Bookstore
- ❏ Direct from O'Reilly
- ❏ Bundled with hardware/software
- ❏ Other _____
- ❏ Computer Store
- ❏ Class/seminar

What operating system do you use?
- ❏ UNIX
- ❏ Windows NT
- ❏ Other _____
- ❏ Macintosh
- ❏ PC(Windows/DOS)

What is your job description?
- ❏ System Administrator
- ❏ Network Administrator
- ❏ Web Developer
- ❏ Other _____
- ❏ Programmer
- ❏ Educator/Teacher

❏ Please send me O'Reilly's catalog, containing a complete listing of O'Reilly books and software.

Name _____   Company/Organization _____

Address _____

City _____   State _____   Zip/Postal Code _____   Country _____

Telephone _____   Internet or other email address (specify network) _____

Nineteenth century wood engraving
of a bear from the O'Reilly &
Associates Nutshell Handbook®
Using & Managing UUCP.

POST CARD

BUSINESS REPLY MAIL
FIRST CLASS MAIL   PERMIT NO. 80   SEBASTOPOL, CA

Postage will be paid by addressee

O'Reilly & Associates, Inc.
101 Morris Street
Sebastopol, CA 95472-9902